A WILDCATS™ HANDBOOK

Stories, Stats and Stuff About Arizona® Basketball

By John Moredich

Copyright © 1996 by The Wichita Eagle and
Beacon Publishing Co., Wichita, Kansas
67201-0820. This publication may not be
reproduced, stored in a retrieval system,
or transmitted in whole or in part, in any
form by any means, electronic, mechanical,
photocopying, recording, or otherwise
without prior permission of The Wichita
Eagle and Beacon Publishing Co.

Printed in the United States of America by
Mennonite Press, Inc.

ISBN 1-880652-80-3

PHOTO CREDITS Photographs were supplied by
Cat Tracks Staff photographers Jim Davidson
and James Orchard, along with Jon Alquist of
the Arizona Alumni Office and the University
of Arizona sports information office.

All names, logos and symbols attributable
to the University of Arizona which appear in
this book are trademarks of the University of
Arizona and have been reproduced with the
permission of the University of Arizona. This
notice is for the purpose of protection of
trademark rights only, and in no way
represents the approval or disapproval of the
text of this book by the University of Arizona.

ACKNOWLEDGMENTS

When writing a book of this magnitude there are more people involved than just the name on the cover. This is the page to give at least some small thanks for help and support.

Because there is no tympany to sound when my time is over as in those numerous award shows, this list could go on forever, but don't worry, it will be cut short.

For starters, thanks must go to *Cat Tracks* Publisher Doug Carr for putting up with all my "half" days during the summer to spend hours in the University of Arizona library. Maybe if I spent that much time with my head in the books while attending the UA my grades would have been better.

Real gratitude goes to a guy who has all the numbers, most of the information and photos regarding Wildcat athletics. That person has been around for what seems like an eternity — Jon Alquist. His knowledge, background material and assistance was an invaluable service in getting this project completed.

For photos, the Cats Handbook production staff must also thank the UA sports information office and the various photographers from Cat Tracks' staff over the years—particularly to Jim Davidson and James Orchard. May there never be motion blur again.

Behind the scenes, but a guy who deserves to be in the forefront because of his dedication to proofing, is John Schuster. He also took over some of the other responsibilities *Cat Tracks* has over the summer.

Much time was spent on the phone with guys who probably had better things to do, but for all the people who gave me a minute, or five or 10 to relive some of their great memories, I hope it is well worth it when people read about your hardships, accomplishments and fortune.

And last, but certainly not least, my family and friends make everything that gets done seem a little better. My mom, sis, and Munch will always be important. And for you other guys I kept blowing off to do work, thanks Anthony, Javier, and Wendy for trying to get me out of the house every now and then.

The old need to know the youth of today is not filled with pure hatred, racism, and evil. There is still hope as long as kids like Elizabeth Scott realize their potential, and reach for the stars.

INTRODUCTION

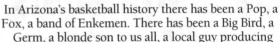

In Arizona's basketball history there has been a Pop, a Fox, a band of Enkemen. There has been a Big Bird, a Germ, a blonde son to us all, a local guy producing better numbers than Alcindor, a guy named Ben (well, let's try to forget about him) and Cool Hand Lute.

That is quite a collection of characters since a basketball was first picked up on the University of Arizona campus in 1897.

Determining a true starting date for basketball in Tucson is a matter of opinion. Some think it began when a team of "Neverwuzzes" defeated the "Hazbins." Others disagree. They point to the time J.F. "Pop" McKale took a team outside the city limits as an appropriate starting date.

Then, there are those who have moved into the Old Pueblo in just the past 13 years or so who know nothing more than Lute Olson. Well, that would be a heck of a start, but there was basketball before Lute.

McKale might not have liked basketball much, but he knew who to hire. When Notre Dame's Knute Rockne suggested some guy named Fred Enke from Louisville, McKale said, "Okay." For 36 years Enke rolled the ball onto the court and told the guys to win. More than 500 times, his players did just that.

And let us not forget Fred "The Fox" Snowden. His charisma was overwhelming, his style unforgettable (especially when one talks about his bellbottom pants). Snowden brought 12,000 fans into the arena every game with his up-and-down style; no shot clock was needed. And Ben...that is a year that needs to be forgotten, but should not be because without Lindsey the Wildcats would never have needed Lute.

Lute's numbers speak, well, for themselves. Two Final Fours, 12 straight NCAA tournament appearances, and the best winning percentage in all of college basketball since 1987.

That is some history, but there is so much more. It is a history of entertainment, in-depth statistical information, heartbreak, tragedy and triumph.

As you read on don't bend the pages, don't use the cover as a coaster and think about what the past might have been and what the future still could be.
— *John Moredich*

TABLE OF CONTENTS

Humble Beginnings

Going to a park or to schools with two relatively straight rims and nets hanging by just a thread would be regarded as primitive conditions to our way of thinking about pickup basketball.

During the emergence of basketball at the University of Arizona these conditions would have been considered heavenly. For starters, basketball rims were a rarity, and nets, well …

PICKUP GAMES In 1897 "organized" pickup games took place on the campus, with the first team recording a 3-1 victory. "Several good plays were made," *The Arizona Daily Wildcat*, the student publication, reported. A contingent of "Shirts" and "Skins" made up the opposition.

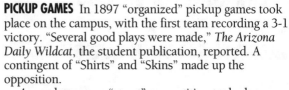

WILDCAT QUIZ

1. Who was the first Wildcat to be drafted by an NBA team?

A year later more "street" competition took place, except the court was dirt — and there was no three-point line. The basketball was bought by a group of students who had scrounged for donations. Too bad there was no lifetime guarantee. The ball lasted just one game because of the poor conditions just in front of the Mines Building.

Good thing it did not rain.

THE FIRST TEAM According to the Arizona basketball media guide, no official games started until the 1904-05 season when Orin A. Kates coached the school to a 1-0-1 record. Morenci's YMCA fell 40-32 to Arizona, while the UA settled for a 19-19 tie against Bisbee's YMCA.

While Kates' name appears as the coach of the 1905-06 team, only intrasquad games were scheduled. One such contest featured the "Neverwuzzers" defeating the "Hazbins" in Herring Hall, Arizona's first gymnasium.

At Herring Hall there were three walls that stood as boundaries with just enough room for fans. Players continually ran into the walls in the cramped quarters, forcing some to wear headgear during practices.

WHO WAS THAT GUY? Arizona records show from 1906-1911 that "Unknown" posted a 10-6 mark. Games were played, captain records were compiled and kept for historical collection, but the coaches were not considered significant. They probably weren't needed against club, high school, and YMCA teams.

When Raymond L. Quigley's name appeared as the X and O guy, Arizona's competition base expanded greatly. Instead of token games against Southern Arizona competition, the school established its first schedule

facing collegiate teams.

During the 1913-14 campaign the Wildcats started their dominance over Arizona State University (back then known as Tempe Normal School). Arizona recorded 41-17 and 15-10 victories.

McKALE'S NAVY If J.F. McKale, otherwise known as "Fritz" or Pop" were alive today he would probably still be trying to get the name changed from Arizona to McKale Stadium. Despite coaching the school's basketball team for seven years, the long time UA sports legend despised the sport.

He preferred football.

To honor McKale's achievements, which were numerous, the school's administration thought it was a "nice gesture" to name the gymnasium after the heralded coach and athletic director. Just why the football stadium wasn't named after him still remains a mystery.

McKale literally brought the sports department from obscurity to national prominence as the school's athletic director from 1914 to 1957 despite a limited budget in the beginning.

McKale arrived in the Old Pueblo in 1911 to coach Tucson High School's football and baseball programs. In his first year THS won the state title in both sports. A year later the wins were coming so easily his opponents

Former athletic director and basketball coach J.F. "Pop" McKale symbolized Wildcat athletics for 43 years.

wanted him out.

A letter-writing campaign to Arizona's administration prompted McKale's hiring as the school's athletic director and coach of—every sport. The position provided him with a $1,700 salary.

There was not much to work with for the former high school coach, who arrived in Tucson via train from Wisconsin. There was no true gymnasium, athletic equipment was sparse, and the outdoor sports were played on rocky conditions with serious need for groundskeepers.

The school did allocate some funds. For the 1915

"Pop" McKale (left) coached basketball for seven years, but preferred directing the football and baseball teams.

season McKale was appropriated $575 for football, $200 for basketball, $40 for tennis, $10 for track, and $10 for baseball. Not exactly an unlimited budget.

He made the most of his responsibilities, recording a 49-12 record in basketball before handing over those duties in 1921. Most of those wins came against YMCA and local teams. Against collegiate competition McKale sported a 13-5 mark.

"In these years our biggest competition was the Bisbee YMCA," McKale said in the *Arizona Daily Wildcat*. "When we beat them we were so happy we shot our rifles off in celebration of the victories."

"Pop" wanted the football facility, not the gymnasium, to be named after him.

In 1917 McKale started playing collegiate foes, taking on the University of New Mexico and the New Mexico State Aggies. Home games were played in Tucson armory gyms.

The style of play was a bit different. Games with scores over 20 were rare.

"The defense was close to assault and battery," McKale said. "Much more body contact was allowed."

There were no flamboyant one-handed dunks, spinning-twisting moves to the basket, or finger rolls in the lane. Everything was more the standard two-handed set shots.

"It was almost a capital crime to shoot a basket with one hand," McKale stated.

Not only did the sports programs prosper under McKale, but traditions were established. It was "Pop" who delivered Button Salmon's words to "Bear Down" when the youngster was on his death bed following a car accident. It was McKale's first football team that played Occidental College, a power in those days, to a tough 14-0 loss, inspiring a reporter to say "they fought like Wildcats." The name stuck.

In 16 football seasons McKale had an 80-32-6 record, including a 60-31-6 mark against college teams. McKale was Arizona's all-time winningest coach until Dick Tomey surpassed the Wildcat legend to open the 1996 season.

1921-23: TARZAN YEARS

After "Pop" McKale said "enough is enough," he looked to James H. Pierce to take over the squad.

The Wildcats finished the first post-McKale season with a 10-2 record against quality competition. The days of schedules loaded with YMCA teams were coming to an end. Arizona played a four-game series against Southern California, winning one game at home and one on the road.

Pierce later became better known for his role as

KING OF THE COURT

James H. Pierce was traveling through Arizona on his trek to Hollywood to become an actor when he met "Pop" McKale, who hired the former Indiana University football center as an assistant coach and eventually the head basketball and track coach.

In August 1921, Pierce signed a $2,500 contract, and guided the basketball program to a 27-5 record over a two-year period. Following the 1924 season he left Tucson—with Hollywood still his aim—and coached Marion Morrison (better known as John Wayne) at Glendale (Calif.) High School. Glendale won a regional championship.

Finally, after several years, Pierce became the last silent film Tarzan. *Tarzan and the Golden Lion* was released in 1927. Pierce finished his film career with 74 movie credits and several jobs on radio, including a Tarzan series with his wife, Joan Burroughs, who played Jane. Pierce died in 1983 and is buried in Shelbyville, Ind., next to his wife. The tombstones read "Tarzan" and "Jane."

"Tarzan." As a coach, however, he preferred Harold Tovrea to Jane. The school's first "star" basketball player led the Wildcats to a 17-3 season as Arizona recorded a total of six wins over UCLA and USC.

TOVREA-A SCORING MACHINE In an age when there was a center jump after every basket, staying in a shooting "zone" was difficult. Tovrea found a way.

With his team averaging 34 points per game, the team's leader scored nearly 16 points an outing. By the time the 1922-23 season was complete, he had scored 316 of the squad's 679 points.

1923-25: TOVREA DOMINATES

Tovrea continued his dominance despite having to cope with constant coaching changes. After the 1923 season, Pierce went off to find fame and some fortune in acting. McKale, the school's athletic director, declined to resurface as coach. He called upon Basil Stanley in 1924.

With Tovrea as the team's captain, Arizona compiled a 14-3 record against the school's toughest schedule to date. The UA played 13 college teams, including USC and California.

Besides a victory over California, the Pacific Coast Champion, Arizona excelled in its own region, earning the bragging rights in the Southwest with victories over teams from the Grand Canyon State, New Mexico, and Texas.

For the next 25 seasons players would find Tovrea's

17.4 point-per-game average as the number to beat. New Mexico Tech found out just how unstoppable Tovrea was when the Wildcat went off for 35 points. Arizona was 43-8 with Tovrea on the floor. In his final two seasons he compiled 44.7 percent of the team's points. Tovrea concluded his career with 612 points and a 16.5 points per game average.

A year later there was neither Tovrea, nor Stanley. Another coaching change was made. This time Walter Davis directed Arizona. Under his guidance the UA went 7-4.

An Enke(ling) of Success

Fred Enke coached the Wildcats for 36 years, compiling a 511-318 record.

By now everybody knows the story behind the "Win one for the Gipper" speech presented by Notre Dame's Knute Rockne. From an Arizona perspective the fable really means very little.

Rockne was, however, partially responsible for winning 511 games for the Wildcats.

It was the famed Fighting Irish coach who recommended Fred Enke, who started his career at South Dakota State and was at Louisville before taking a train to Tucson for a job interview with Arizona's "Pop" McKale.

"I took the train out to Tucson and Slony (Slonaker) and McKale met me, took me around the campus and then out to Wetmore Pool. The pool was a big thing in Tucson in those days," Enke related in the book *They Fought Like Wildcats* by Abe Chanin. "Viewing the campus was a shock to me because there was no gymnasium. Here I was to be the basketball coach, see, and there was just that little Herring Hall. I decided to take the challenge. I wired my wife that we were going to move to Tucson, that I'd taken the job as basketball coach and assistant in football at a salary of $3,000."

Rockne had been impressed by Enke, a former all-Big Ten standout in football and basketball at Minnesota, while he was assisting at a football clinic at Notre Dame. McKale called requesting a good candidate for a job that had been occupied by three different coaches in the last four years. McKale wanted stability.

Enke started in 1925 and finished 36 years later with a 511-318 overall record and a 402-300 mark against collegiate competition. Upon his retirement in 1961, Enke was one of only five college coaches who had posted 500 victories. He had won 11 Border Conference titles in the process.

"Fred truly was a character," said former Enke player George Rountree. "He was certainly one of the best coaches in his era. There was an august group of colleagues who thought a great deal of him. He was immensely successful and a great credit to the University of Arizona."

Enke's recruiting philosophy was simple — get the best guys available in the area. There was little choice. Unlike today, there were no summer camps sponsored by Nike, Adidas, or Reebok in places like Indianapolis, Las Vegas, New Jersey, and Colorado Springs.

Players showed up.

"I don't even think I talked to him," said Bob Mueller, who played from 1956-58. "There was no such thing as recruiting back then. I came to Arizona because I didn't have too many choices. Arizona had a better reputation in-state as a teaching college."

The players who came needed a basic working knowledge of the game, or else.

"He was the type of coach who threw the ball out and said, 'Go play.' He expected you to know the fundamentals," Rountree said. "He recruited players who played for coaches that were fundamentally sound. He was very impatient with anyone who did not do what was expected from them."

Enke's best stretch occurred following World War II (1945-1951), when his teams won 75 percent of their games (132-45), six Border championships, played in Madison Square Garden at the National Invitational Tournament, and made the NCAA playoffs for the first time in school history. In the process he also coached in such historic gymnasiums as the Cow Palace in San

The recently established Fred A. Enke Plaza stands just outside McKale Center.

Francisco and Convention Hall in Philadelphia.

Enke did have his critics. He had only one winning record during his last 10 years. Many thought he was too stubborn to go against a man-to-man defense when a zone was needed or to know when to take players out because of fatigue. But for 36 years he roamed the Arizona sidelines, winning 511 games for Arizona.

1926-1932: BEAR DOWN GYM

The highlight of the early Enke years was beginning play at Bear Down Gym on January 21, 1927. The arena, regarded as a high-class facility in those days, combined with Enke's background, generated excitement for basketball.

John "Button" Salmon's last words continue to be a part of Arizona's athletic history.

"TELL THEM...
TELL THE TEAM
TO
BEAR DOWN"

JOHN BUTTON SALMON
1904 ——— 1926

IN HONOR OF ALL
WILDCAT LETTERWINNERS

The Arizona campus has changed significantly in the past few years. Before the state-of-the-art McKale Center or the garage parking lots and the high-rise classrooms, "Bear Down" Gym and the football stadium were in a sparse area of campus.

After a 6-7 season to open his Arizona coaching career, the Wildcats slowly began to excel in the region. Led by team captains Frank Brookshier and George Sorenson, the next three years produced records of 13-4, 13-3 and 19-4.

By the 1929-30 season, Arizona was becoming a force. The Wildcats tied New Mexico for the Southwestern Championship with a 15-6 record. Arizona went 3-1 against Arizona State that year. Neil Goodman led the team in scoring with 175 points, an 8.4 clip.

1932-33: DEPRESSION CONQUERED

The Great Depression struck the United States, but there were plenty of reasons for smiles in Tucson with Enke's team racking up a 19-5 overall record and a 7-3 mark in Border action against the likes of ASU, NAU, New Mexico State, and New Mexico. West Texas State, Hardin-Simmons, Texas Tech, and Texas Western (UTEP) would later enter the league. Jack Raffs led the team with 185 points in 23 games, an eight point average.

LEG ROOM LIMITED The team's travel budget did not call for first-class airline tickets, stays in luxurious resorts,

In 1925, prior to Arizona's football game with New Mexico A&M, football player Button Salmon was taken to the hospital following a car accident. J.F. "Pop" McKale asked Salmon if there was anything he wanted to tell the team. Salmon replied: "Tell them … Tell them to Bear Down."

THE BEAR FACTS

From 1925 until McKale Center was built in 1973, the Arizona basketball team called Bear Down Gym home.

The Arizona Board of Regents was a little slow in accepting that fact since it officially named "Bear Down Gym" 10 years after the last varsity game was played there.

In its 45 years of service (save the seasons when it was occupied by the Navy during World War II), the old gym created havoc for opponents. Former Wildcat Bob Mueller (1956-58) considered Bear Down Gym "a seven- or eight-point advantage" every time.

The following is a listing of the prominent events that took place in Bear Down Gym:

1925 The Clinton Campbell Construction Corporation of Phoenix receives a contract to build Bear Down Gym, at a cost of $130,000.

1926 In July construction is completed.

On October 30 a homecoming dance christens the structure.

1927 January 7 — The first game is played. Arizona's varsity team defeats its freshmen 33-20.

January 21 — Arizona's 29-18 victory over Arizona State College is the dedication game. Waldo Dicus leads the Wildcats with 10 points.

February 24-26—The first state high school basketball tournament takes place. Gilbert defeats Safford, 19-18, in the championship game.

December — The Chain Gang, the junior men's honorary

group, sponsors a fund-raising dance in the gym, raising enough money to paint "Bear Down" on the roof to honor the last words of Button Salmon.

1928 January — "Bear Down" is painted on the roof, unofficially making the building "Bear Down Gym."

1929 Arizona wins nine straight games at home after opening with two consecutive losses.

1930 February 10 — Arizona's 29-16 loss to DePaul represents the first intersectional game played.

1932 Thanks to its home dominance, Arizona wins its first Border Conference title.

1942-44 Gym becomes a dormitory for a Navy training school. Arizona plays games at Tucson High School.

1945 December 14 — Arizona defeats Williams Air Force Base to begin an 81-game home-court winning streak.

1948 Arizona sets a single game scoring record with a 93-50 victory over the West Texas (now UTEP) Miners.

1951 January 29 — Arizona upsets No. 2 ranked Long Island University, 62-61, in front of 4,650 fans. The Wildcats finish the year 14-0 at home, 24-6 overall.

1952 December 8 — Arizona's 81-game home court winning streak ends with a 76-57 loss to Kansas State.

1954 February 1 — Hadie Redd

leads Arizona with 26 points in an 87-74 victory over No. 17 Bradley.

December 6 — Fred Enke, in his 30th year, records his 500th career victory in an 86-81 triumph over Kansas State.

1955 March 2 — In a 104-103 loss to Arizona State, the Wildcats score over 100 points in Bear Down Gym for the first time. Eli (Teddy) Lazovich also set a gym record with 38 points.

1956 February 1—Bill Reeves sets a record (that still stands) with 26 rebounds against UC-Santa Barbara in a 68-53 win.

1959 A 79-38 loss to Santa Clara is the worst for Arizona in Bear Down Gym. In the 41-point defeat, Arizona makes 12 of 63 shots from the field.

Arizona records its first losing season in the building, going 3-8. The team finishes 4-22.

1960 February 6 — Ernie McCray scores 46 points (a single-game record that still stands) in a 104-84 victory over Los Angeles State. McCray makes 16 field goals and 14 free throws.

January 13 — Arizona records the most points scored and the biggest victory margin in Bear Down Gym in a 118-66 rout of Eastern New Mexico.

1961 Arizona is 11-15 at home in the final season under Fred Enke, who retires after 36 years with a Wildcat coaching record of 510-326. Enke's record in Bear Down Gym is 297-85, a .778 winning percentage.

1962 January 4 — Joe Skaisgir scores 44 points and sets a school record with 17 field goals in a 101-62 victory over Hardin-Simmons.

January 31 — Skaisgir ties Bill Reeves' single-game rebounding record with 26 boards against Los Angeles State.

1965 January 28 — Arizona upsets eighth-ranked San Francisco, 71-56.

Arizona finishes the season 12-1 at home, the team's best record since the 1950-51 season.

1972 Only seven games are played in Bear Down Gym. Non-conference games were scheduled for the Tucson Community Center. The Wildcats are 3-4 at Bear Down, just their second losing season in the facility.

Bruce Larson, after 11 years of coaching Arizona, had a 101-34 record at Bear Down Gym

1973 January 19 — Arizona defeats UC-Santa Barbara, 79-77, in the last varsity game played in the building.

Fred Snowden has won all seven games he coached in Bear Down Gym.

Arizona produced a 405-119 record in Bear Down Gym, a 77.3 percentage. There were eight undefeated seasons with the best marks being 14-0 campaigns in 1946, 48 and 51. There were two losing seasons, 1959 and 1972.

— Compiled by Jon Alquist, UA Alumni Association

and reservations at the finest restaurants.

Instead of United or American Airlines, the squad took Enke's two-door Chevrolet and Doc Johnson's two-door Ford. Four players were crammed in each car, including the coaches and the manager. It was a tight fit.

Harold Warnock and Vincent Byrne were described as "beanpoles," while Howard Abbott and Davis Filbrun were all-conference football players. Johnson was the heavyweight boxing champion of the conference. Warnock described trips through the desert from Tucson to Los Angeles as "tedious." Hotels cost $3 per day. Boos Brothers Cafeteria was the dining establishment of choice: "All you can eat for 99 cents." Pregame meals were supplied by opponents like Pomona, Occidental, and LaVerne in dining halls, but an Enke idiosyncrasy required baked apples before games.

"All-you-can-eat records were set every night," Warnock said.

WILDCAT QUIZ

2. *What was J.F. McKale's nickname other than "Pop"?*

1933-34: GIVE ME A RIDE

The basketball program's first road trip outside of Arizona, California, and New Mexico was noteworthy for distances traveled, but in terms of winning a second Border championship, it was a disaster.

The scheduled 15-day excursion can be blamed, at least partially, for the Wildcats' losing the conference championship to Texas Tech. Despite winning 11 of the final 12 games of the year Arizona fell short at 18-9 overall and 9-3 in league action.

Vince Byrne led the team with 10.3 points, upping his average to 12.6 during Border play. Byrne, George "Doc" Johnson and Gene Filburm were first-team all-conference players.

THE TRIP THAT WOULDN'T END On December 23, 1933 Enke and his traveling squad left Tucson on a chartered bus for the school's first games outside of the Southwest region. A nine-game, 15-day trip was in store.

Plans changed.

Games were slated against a local group from El Paso, followed by contests at Oklahoma City University, Southwestern College of Winfield in Kansas, Drake, Purdue, Illinois Wesleyan, DePaul, Notre Dame, and Saint Louis. Arizona won three, including victories over Oklahoma City and Drake.

That was the good news.

After the final game the bus broke down outside St. Louis. Team members hitchhiked until they reached Tulsa, where another bus was chartered.

On the way back from Oklahoma City, that bus broke

down. The team was stuck for days trying to beg, borrow, or steal transportation back to Tucson.

On January 14 the trip ended. Bone weary, the Wildcats had less than 24 hours to prepare for Border favorite Texas Tech. (At least the game was in Bear Down Gym.) Arizona lost.

1934-41: CONSISTENCY PAYS OFF

A common ingredient in all of Enke's teams was consistency.

In the 1935-36 season, Arizona was 16-7 and won the Border crown with a league mark of 11-5. The Wildcats finished second a year later as Lorry Di Grazia and Tom Greenfield earned second-team all-league status. The only loss outside of Border play was to Pacific Coast Conference (predecessor to the Pac-10) Champion Stanford, which featured the nation's Player of the Year, Hank Luisetti.

Luisetti is credited with establishing the jump shot. Despite that unofficial patent, Arizona held him to one point in the first half. Luisetti scored 11 points after intermission and helped Stanford post a 44-28 win.

George Jordan led the next two teams with his scoring prowess, averaging 11.2 points on the 1938-39 team, which finished 12-11 overall, 8-10 in league play. The 6-foot-7 center accounted for 9.9 points in 1939-40. That squad made a tremendous turnaround after losing the first six games of the season. Arizona tied New

The post World War II era was quite successful thanks largely to the talents of John Padelford, George Genung, Thomas Ballantyne, Fred Enke Jr., and Link Richmond.

Mexico State for first place in the Border with a 15-10 overall mark, a 12-4 record in league play.

Vince Cullen was the spark in an 11-7, 9-6 season with a 31 point outburst against New Mexico during the 1940-41 campaign.

THE WAR YEARS

Following the December 7, 1941, Japanese raid on Pearl Harbor, basketball was the last thing anybody across the country really cared about. Some schools gave up the game entirely — at least for awhile. Others used the sport as a diversion from the harsh reality and dangers apparent throughout the world.

THE 1941-42 SEASON The Arizona basketball program continued, and by the end of World War II had garnered an even larger following.

The 1941-42 season was a disappointment in terms of the 9-13 record (Enke's second losing season in 17 years), but better years were to follow. The Wildcats were 6-10 in the nine-team Border Conference.

Vince Cullen led the squad with a 10.4 per game average. Bob Ruman, a three-sport standout, averaged 10.3 points. Another significant contributor also made his appearance—Morris K. (Mo) Udall. Udall not only turned out to be an excellent basketball player but a world-class politician.

THE 1942-43 SEASON No longer did the Wildcats call Bear Down Gym home. The United States Navy did because of the war efforts. The arena was used as a training site.

Arizona's team was shipped to Tucson High School — just a half-mile from the campus. The Border Conference also shut down. But wartime restrictions didn't prevent the continuation of rivalries — Arizona posted a 22-2 record, which included victories against league foes Northern Arizona, Arizona State, and UTEP.

Bob Ruman took the scoring honors for the second year in a row, posting 11.4 points per game, while Vince Cullen scored 10 points a night. This squad, which lost only to Arizona State, 41-39, and Texas Tech, 47-35, could also play defense. Arizona averaged 58.8 points, while limiting teams to 38.8 points.

THE 1943-44 SEASON The college basketball scene closed down. The only games in town were against regional military squads. Arizona fared well, recording a 12-2 record. George Genung excelled, leading the team in scoring (13.7) and in rebounds.

WILDCAT QUIZ

3. Can you name the five buildings Arizona played home basketball games in over the course of its history?

THE 1944-45 SEASON With men flying off to battle, the Wildcats were left with one returning letterman. Enke's roster consisted of underage and draft-deferred men and veterans.

The group did play games in Bear Down Gym after the U.S. Navy pulled back from the training facility. An 18-game slate was formed with clashes set against Arizona State and NAU to finish the season with a 7-11 record. Freshman Jimmy Steele led the team in scoring with 12.1 points.

YEARS OF PROSPERITY

The string of successes that Coach Lute Olson has achieved at Arizona over the past decade can only be rivaled in Wildcat lore with the six-season run that Enke had following the end of wartime hostilities.

Over those years the Wildcats won 75 percent of their games (132-45), appeared in the school's first postseason playoff, won six Border Conference titles, and made the school's initial trek East.

The names of many of the greats during this time span may not be on the tip of the tongue these days, but the Udall brothers, Link Richmond, Marvin Borodkin, Leo Johnson, and Roger Johnson (no relation) were the Sean Elliotts, Steve Kerrs, and Damon Stoudamires of the '40s and '50s.

THE 1945-46 SEASON Arizona had become a regional force many years earlier, but by the time this season was complete fans from across the country knew there was more to Arizona than cactus and the Grand Canyon. A high standard of basketball was being demonstrated.

The 1945-46 team: (From left to right) Standing: Coach Fred Enke, manager Leon Lampner, Link Richmond, Thomas Ballantyne, Andrew Troutz, William Elder, George Genung, Hillard Crum Jr., manager Claude Ricks. Kneeling: Fred Enke Jr., Louis Silverstein, Stewart Udall, Marvin Borodkin, John McIntyre, Harold Goodman, and Sam Stevens.

Arizona won 23 of its last 24 games, the lone defeat coming at NAU in overtime. The team also started the school's longest home-court winning streak.

With a 25-5 overall record and the first Border championship since the war had begun, Arizona was rewarded with an invitation to the National Invitational Tournament at Madison Square Garden in New York City. The NIT at that time was more prominent than the NCAA tournament.

NEW YORK, NEW YORK Arizona was among an elite eight-team NIT field.

The 11-man traveling team left Sunday, March 10, for the Big Apple. After a one-day stopover in Chicago for a practice session, the Wildcats arrived at Grand Central Station on Wednesday. It was the farthest a Wildcat team had traveled since the school's nationally prominent polo team went east in the 1930s. (The longest distance previously played by the basketball team was at Notre Dame.)

Being paired against Kentucky meant doom. Link Richmond and Fred W. Enke, Jr. did their best to keep Arizona within striking range, but a 16-1 deficit pretty much set the tone. The UA crept to within 51-42 with 12 minutes left in the game, but ultimately fell 77-53 to top-seeded UK.

Richmond led all scorers with 21 points. Enke had 18 points, 14 in the second half. Kentucky went on to defeat Rhode Island in the championship game.

THE STREAK BEGINS Getting opponents scheduled for games in McKale Center in the late 1980s was difficult because visitors faced almost-certain defeat in the building. From 1987-92 the Wildcats won 71 straight games.

That was impressive.

Even more grandiose was the 81-game win streak at

Instead of staying in Arizona, the 1945-46 team went to New York's Madison Square Garden to play Kentucky in the National Invitational Tournament. No UA basketball team had ever traveled that far before. The squad lost to Kentucky but finished the year with a 25-5 record. In the process Arizona began what turned out to be an 81-game home-court winning streak.

TICKETS ANYBODY?

It was difficult getting a good seat, or any standing room at all, during these heydays. There were too many fans, and not enough tickets. Announcements were made:

"Bear Down" Gym seating capacity:

1,550	Main Floor
1,200	Balconies
2,750	Total

The increased student registration makes it necessary to tentatively limit the public sale of tickets as follows:

416 Reserved Seats . . . . . .@$1.20
(Main Floor-between baskets)
250 General Admission . .@$0.75
(Main Floor-behind baskets)

Bear Down Gym that started on December 14 with a 50-47 victory over Williams Air Force Base. It would be six years before the Wildcats lost at home again.

HONORS Richmond, the team's top scorer with 312 points in 21 games (14.8 average), along with Enke and Tim Ballantyne, were first-team all-Border selections. Marvin Borodkin and George Genung were second-team all-league. Not named to any honors team but quite effective both on the court and later in national government, was starting guard Stewart Udall, a future congressman, state representative, and U.S. Secretary of the Interior.

From 1949-51 Leo Johnson spearheaded Arizona's league dominance and propelled the UA to NCAA tournament appearances.

THE 1946-47 SEASON Combined with the fame from the previous year and the return of most everybody from not only that squad, but many from the 1942-43 team that had posted a 22-2 record, it appeared the Wildcats would be dominant.

They were.

A second consecutive Border Conference title was won with a 21-3 overall mark and a 14-3 record in league action. Richmond set a school record in the process with 428 points.

SCOUTING REPORT The 1946-47 team media preview contained a little more pizzazz — and unusual descriptions — than sports information departments provide for sportswriters and broadcasters today. For example:

■ Junior Crum — "center, dangerous with overhand and 'ball on platter' shots."

■ Fred Enke, Jr. — "forward and an excellent guard, fearless ball passer and high scorer from under the basket."

■ Harold Goodman — "forward, diminutive player with ambitious heart to win."

■ Link Richmond — "forward, prize cat of the Arizona lair. Knows what is happening every second all over the floor."

■ Morris Udall — "forward and center, high-scoring player and top floor worker. Letterman on Arizona's varsity 1941-42. St. Johns High School, second-team all-state 1940."

■ Stewart Udall — "guard, fast, accurate shot, and dependable guard. Senior, letterman on Arizona varsity 1941-42, all-conference second team 1940. From St. Johns High School."

THE 1947-48 SEASON After a third straight Border title with a 17-10 overall record and a 12-4 mark in league play, the Wildcats received their first NCAA playoff berth.

Arizona played Baylor, a team it had defeated in the regular season, 62-54, in a best-of-three District VI series. Arizona was not as fortunate in the playoffs, losing two in a row, 65-59, and, 64-54. (Baylor wound up losing to Kentucky in the NCAA championship game.)

Morris Udall led the team in scoring with 13.3 points. He scored 14.4 in conference action. Udall and Fred Enke, Jr. were all-Border Conference first-team members.

WILDCAT QUIZ

4. What were the nine teams participating in the Border Conference by 1942?

THE 1948-49 SEASON Border teams simply had no answer for the Wildcats, as the team won a fourth-straight league title. Arizona posted a 17-11 overall record and a 13-3 mark in league play.

The Wildcats competed in NCAA postseason play for the second consecutive year. Arizona received a bit of revenge from the previous year at the four-team District VI playoffs with a 55-47 victory over Baylor. The Wildcats lost to Arkansas, however, 65-44.

TOP SCORERS Leon Blevins led Arizona with 13.7 points per game and first-team Border honors. Hilliard (Junior) Crum, a second-teamer, scored 13 points.

LINK ENDS RICH(MOND) TENURE A leg injury during his senior football season hampered Richmond's play throughout the 1948-49 basketball campaign, but few finished with a better career. He concluded his eligibility with 1,246 points, a school record that would stay intact until 1960.

Richmond was the first player to score over 1,000 career points. He was a two-time Border first-team player and Arizona's only six-year letterman. In addition to basketball, Richmond excelled in baseball and football. In 1946 Richmond led the baseball team with a .400 batting average. He was also Arizona's leading hitter in 1949.

THE 1949-50 SEASON Arizona finished the season ranked Number 15 in The Associated Press poll, made another appearance in the NIT with a 24-5 record, and went 14-2 in winning a fifth-straight Border crown.

The Wildcats had two 10-game winning streaks. Following the first run Arizona lost, 61-54, at Loyola. The season came to a conclusion with a 73-66 setback to LaSalle.

STARTING FIVE Leon Blevins and Bob Honea were the starters at the forward spots, with Paul Penner at center and Leo and Roger Johnson as guards.

The UA was led by Blevins, who set a single-season school record with 452 points and a 14.9 scoring average. Blevins was named to the UPI all-Coast and the Colliers Magazine all-district VI teams.

THE 1950-51 SEASON Imagine what John Wooden would have done if he had to start a team with everybody on his roster standing 6-5 or smaller.

Six feet, five inches.

There would have been no Lew Alcindor, Bill Walton, or other famous Bruin All-Americans.

The Arizona team that took to the court in 1950 did so without excuses. The Wildcats were small, but feisty. Short, but cunning. It was a team of "midgets" by today's standards. Despite everybody measuring in at under 77 inches, Arizona sported a team that many believe could rank among the top three to ever play in Tucson.

NUMBERS SPEAK FOR THEMSELVES Arizona extended its home-court winning streak to 79 games, posted a 15-1 Border record (its sixth straight league title) and concluded the year with a 22-6 mark.

The four regular season losses were by a combined 11 points. Arizona finished the campaign ranked 12th in the nation.

POINT SHAVING In a game Enke declared as "our greatest basketball victory," the Wildcats defeated City College of New York (CCNY), the defending NCAA and NIT champions, in Madison Square Garden, 41-38. Arizona also beat scrutiny.

"The Midgets." Despite nobody on the 1950-51 roster standing taller than 6-foot-5, this Wildcat group won the school's sixth straight Border title and defeated high-powered schools like CCNY and Long Island. Leo and Roger Johnson (no relation) led the way.

Following the game an investigation took place. CCNY players were accused of point shaving. Evidence later proved the Beavers did not lose this one fair and square.

"We would go up and then they would catch us, and then we would get the lead again and they never caught us," said Leo Johnson, a member of that team. "We didn't know how they played. We were feeling pretty good about ourselves. Later when they told us about the point shaving we were all pretty disappointed."

There was no time to celebrate the monumental win. Arizona packed its bags and traveled to West Virginia days later to face a Mountaineer team with a 42-game home winning streak. The UA won 68-67. It was a fun trip home.

Arizona became the first Border team to sweep the three West Texas schools away from home. West Texas State, Texas Tech, and Hardin-Simmons all fell to the Wildcats on consecutive nights in January.

Arizona finally had the opportunity to celebrate a big win at home, defeating national power Long Island, 62-61, with a record 4,651 people (in the 3,600 capacity gym) watching.

THE SMALL GIANTS The collective talents of Roger and Leo Johnson, combined with Bob Honea, played much taller than their listed heights.

These little guys wound up defeating teams by 14.2 points per game and unbelievably still hold the school record for rebounds and rebound margin per game — 59.5 and 19.2, respectively.

In comparison, the 1990-91 Wildcat team of seven-footer Ed Stokes, 6-11 Brian Williams, and 6-10 Sean Rooks grabbed only 40.6 rebounds a game.

"An asterisk almost has to be used because back then there were so many shots missed. That meant

IT'S OVER

After 81 straight victories the Wildcats were finally bested in Bear Down Gym. Kansas State pounded Arizona 76-57. The UA also fell to West Texas State 59-57 on February 7 to end a 59-game home winning streak against conference competition.

The following are the longest home winning streaks in NCAA history:

Team	Games	Years
Kentucky	129	1943-55
St. Bonaventure	99	1948-61
UCLA	98	1970-76
Arizona	81	1945-51
Marquette	81	1967-73
Lamar	80	1978-84
Long Beach State	75	1968-74
UNLV	72	1974-78
Arizona	71	1987-92

more rebounds," Bill Kemmeries said. "We would shoot 20 percent. If you shoot 40 percent today you are going to lose."

DOUBLE FIRST ROUND LOSSES A heralded regular season quickly faded with first-round defeats. There was a double-whammy with losses in NIT and NCAA postseason games (teams were permitted to play in both tournaments).

Arizona fell 74-68 in the first round of the NIT to Dayton, which went on to play in the championship game. The Wildcats then lost 61-59 to Kansas State in NCAA play. No. 3 rated Kansas State had the home-court advantage, a 16-point halftime lead, and a 23-point edge before the Wildcats responded in the second half.

Despite cutting the lead to one with 1:30 left, Arizona could not get over the hump.

"It was just an honor for us to play (in the first rounds). It is not like it is now if Lute (Olson) loses in the first round. There were no expectations on us," Kemmeries said. "There are high expectations on Lute."

JOHNSON & JOHNSON Leo and Roger Johnson played with an uncanny sense of one another.

Roger was named the captain of the Border all-star team and was a third-team all-American by *The Sporting News* and the Helms Foundation.

Leo was an all-conference and all-American honorable mention player after setting a school record in a season with 373 rebounds. The 6-4 guard from Safford averaged 12.5 rebounds per game. That remains the second highest average in the record books. Leo also had 146 assists. Upon graduation he played for college all-star teams and toured with the Harlem Globetrotters.

1951-52: RACIAL EQUALITY

All good things must come to an end. Not only did Kansas State break through for a blowout victory in Bear Down Gym, but the Wildcats' streak of Border championships evaporated.

Roger Johnson was the only significant returner from 1950-51. Three of the team's top four scorers and the four best rebounders all left, leaving little for Enke.

The result was an overall record of 11-16. Arizona was 6-8 in Border action, good for a fourth place finish in league play.

THE DEBUT OF HADIE REDD Back in 1950 a black man playing for a institution was unspeakable. Many schools

Arizona broke the color barrier when Fred Enke accepted Phoenix Carver High School standout Hadie Redd for the 1951 squad. Despite racial injustices, Redd emerged as one of the top players in early Wildcat history. He averaged 13.6 points and 9.4 rebounds his senior season.

stayed away from such situations. Enke watched Hadie Redd play and said, "Welcome."

Redd, a 6-3 freshman from Carver High School in Phoenix, was accepted immediately by his teammates. Averaging 7.8 points in 17 games, and leading the team in rebounds with 7.5 per game, has a way of blinding many to color.

Before Redd concluded his career few argued his importance to the program or his caliber of play despite constant scrutiny and profanity laden crowds.

"I remember the Mayo Hotel in Oklahoma State. It was downtown," Bill Reeves said. "There were no

BLACK DILEMMAS

It took decades for acceptance between black and white cultures, and some believe a line still exists, but in the 1950s and early '60s there was clearly a dividing point.

Nobody felt the division in Tucson more than the first two African-American basketball players on the Arizona roster.

"If you take any of these kids off of our teams today and put them into that era they would never have made it," said Bill Reeves, a Wildcat player from 1955-57. "They would never have been able to put up with the crap guys like Hadie Redd and Ernie McCray had to put up with."

In 1951, Redd joined the Wildcat team, but he was still an outsider, especially on road trips when Coach Fred Enke had to locate other sleeping and eating arrangements for his 6-foot-3 freshman from Carver High School in Phoenix. Restaurants and even more hotels refused service to the youngster.

"Fred had to set up homes with black families on the road for Redd," George Rountree (1953-55) recalls. "He never really let anything bother him. It probably did. It had do, but he was very well accepted by our team."

One occasion did rattle Redd.

"We were playing in Lubbock, against Texas Tech," Rountree said. "It was a 78-foot court. There were small borders all around the sidelines. There were about 800 to 1,200 people in the stands. Before the game started somebody yelled from the top row some horrible thing I won't repeat. It was something like, 'You SOB, go back to Tucson. We don't want you people here.' He was a non-factor in the game. That really got to him. There is no question it had a horrible impact on him."

That was a rare exception in which Redd wavered on the court. As a freshman he averaged 7.8 points and led the team in rebounding with 7.5 after 17 games before becoming academically ineligible. Two years later he

Ernie McCray, Arizona's second black player, established himself as a scorer and a role model for other African-Americans.

Regency or Hyatts. There was a revolving door. The team gets out of the vans — we didn't have buses — and we get out and I'm with Hadie. I'm walking behind him through the revolving door. There was a big black doorman. He is standing inside and grabs Hadie and says, 'Boy, you can't come in here.' He went right back out the revolving door. So, he's out there on the curb. They arranged for a black doctor for him to stay with."

NOTABLES Roger Johnson, Arizona's first all-American, became the second player to score over 1,000 points, finishing his career with 1,046. As a senior he tallied

became one of the first Wildcats to score over 300 points in a season. As a senior he led the team in scoring and rebounding with 13.6 points and 9.4 rebounds.

Redd paved the way for other black players. McCray took advantage of that opportunity — and then made others.

Following his 1959-60 senior season, McCray owned 13 school records, including a 23.9 point-per-game average. He scored 46 points against Cal State-Los Angeles; attempted 257 free throws during the season, making 177 of them; and set the mark with 14 converted free throws in one game.

McCray earned Border Conference all-star status and was an honorable mention all-American before being drafted by the Cincinnati Royals of the NBA.

McCray did all of this despite constant harassment.

"There was once we went on the Texas swing. In Abilene, I believe, we sat down to eat and the owner, or somebody like that, told us they couldn't serve us," Bob Mueller said. "Fred asked, 'Why not?' He said because we don't serve black persons here. We all got up and left."

McCray persevered.

"The University of Arizona, through its athletes, became my refuge from the realities faced by a little black boy growing up in Tucson in the '40s and '50s," McCray wrote later. "Cheering wildly as spindlelegged Eddie Wolgast twisted and turned through a host of would-be tacklers, or as Fred Batiste flat-out blew by them, or as Oscar Carrillo ran over them. That eased the pain of having someone say to me: 'We don't serve Negros here,' when I didn't want any Negros, just a hamburger and a Coke.

"Sitting back, enjoying watching Link Richmond fake a defender out of his jock, took the sting out of being called 'eight ball,' or being harassed by a cop who asks, 'What are you doing around here, boy?' while I'm standing in front of my house, minding my own business, praying that this dude will leave me alone. To escape that real world of my youth I would sit on one of the UA's lawns and imagine scoring baskets by the dozens before a multitude of screaming fans. My dreams came true."

Ernie McCray set a standard, not only for minority players to follow, but everybody — especially in terms of scoring.

13.6 points and 6.9 rebounds per game. Johnson also led the team in assists with 86.

Kemmeries, a Tucson native, led the team with 14.1 points per game and a 40.8 field goal percentage. The 6-2 forward became an all-conference player, leading the league in scoring with 18.2 points per outing. Against Hardin-Simmons on February 16, Kemmeries scored a career-high 32 points, taking 32 shots and making 14 in the process.

1952-53: OFF THE MARK

After an off-year, Enke got the ball rolling again with a share of the Border title with Hardin-Simmons. Arizona's league record of 11-3 was worthy, but the team's 13-11 overall record is a little misleading.

TOUGH LOSSES Mixed in with those defeats were losses to LaSalle, the 1952 and 1954 NCAA Champion, and 1954 NCAA runner-up Bradley. In both games George Rountree proved to be worthy of the national caliber of play, scoring 18 against No. 1 ranked LaSalle and 19 against Bradley.

HEADS OR TAILS Arizona appeared to be going nowhere with a 3-8 record to open the year, but five straight conference wins and eight of 10 victories midway through the season forced a playoff.

Upon tying Hardin-Simmons for first with three consecutive wins in the regular season, a coin flip was used to decide where a one-game conference playoff would take place to decide the league's lone NCAA tournament berth.

Arizona lost the flip, and then the game, 67-61, in overtime.

TOP PLAYERS Kemmeries led Arizona with 13.8 points per game to earn second-team all-conference honors. Rountree averaged 10.5 points, while Eli Lazovich grabbed 6.5 rebounds a contest.

1953-54: 300 POINT CLUB

Despite two wins against NCAA Final Four teams the Wildcats finished the year 14-10 overall, 8-4 in Border play and tied for second with West Texas State.

Arizona defeated Bradley 87-74 to avenge an earlier 79-55 loss and then upset USC 57-55 in Bear Down Gym. Bradley lost to LaSalle in the championship game.

The Wildcats were led by 6-6 center John Bruner and Redd, a second-team Border player. Redd averaged 13.2 points and seven rebounds. Joining Redd on the "300" point club was Eli (Ted) Lazovich.

1954-55: ENKE GETS 500TH

Darrell Blankinship's two-handed shot directly under the basket with three seconds left keyed a 73-72 victory over West Texas State early in the season. That was one of the last bright points as the Wildcats fell to 8-17 overall, 3-9 in league action.

ROAD WOES There was no long home winning streak to boast about, but Arizona was still dangerous in Bear Down. The Wildcats pulled off wins over national powers Kansas State and Bradley, and Border champion West Texas State.

On the road Arizona struggled to a 1-12 record.

A free-throw shooting display of mythical proportions took place in 1953. The NCAA had to rewrite its records for most personal fouls in a game by both teams (84), by one team (Arizona-50), for most free throws attempted by one team (Northern Arizona-79), and for both teams (130). Ten players fouled out, six from Arizona, as the Wildcats won, 90-70. (Northern Arizona, incidentally, made 12-of-96 field goal attempts, a 12.5 percentage.)

An 86-81 victory on December 6, 1954, over Kansas State in Bear Down Gym proved to be the 500th win of Enke's career. Later, through checks, the NCAA decided 109 victories were not against collegiate competition. Enke would conclude his career with 511 victories, 402 collegiate wins.

COLOR BLIND Enke was notorious for being color-blind, which hampered his fashion statements, particularly on the road. Guard George Rountree had a solution.

"We were in Salt Lake City and you have to know that Fred's wife packed his bags and put his clothes together that would match. I knew he was color-blind. I went into his room and changed things around. He came out in the most garish outfit of clothes that he had ever put on. People were almost laughing at him. He figured out what happened and said, 'Damn you Rountree, you have done it to me again. I ought to not start you tonight,'" Rountree recalled, with a chuckle.

NOTABLES A 104-103 loss to Arizona State in the final game of the season proved to be memorable for Lazovich, who set a Bear Down record with 38 points. It was the first time the Wildcats had scored over 100 points.

Lazovich tied the score with 16 seconds remaining to send the game into overtime. Redd added 20 points, while Jim Brower contributed 15. Redd led the team in scoring with 13.6 points and 9.4 rebounds.

Arizona was one of the few teams in the Western Athletic Conference that had a representative racial mixture, as evidenced by the 1957-58 team. Pictured are Warren Ridge, Ed Nymeyer, Mitchell, Fred Enke, Bob Mueller, and Ernie McCray.

1955-61: INDIVIDUALS PERSEVERE

During the late stages of Enke's career it was obvious the fire was dwindling after 30-plus years of the constant routine. Arizona's highest finish in Border play was

third place.

There was no lower single game than a 119-45 loss at Utah during the 1955-56 season, the worst defeat in school history.

By the conclusion of the 1960-61 season Enke called it quits, giving the job to Bruce Larson, a former player and a coach groomed for just this moment.

Team accomplishments became secondary to some highlight-reel individual feats, such as:

■ 1955-56: Junior Bill Reeves set a standing school record with 13.2 rebounds per game. He also set a single-game mark with 26 boards versus UC-Santa Barbara. Ed "Pudge" Nymeyer became the third Wildcat to score over 400 points. Co-captain Bill Wagner later became one of Arizona's first Olympians, competing for Mexico in the 1960 Rome Olympics.

■ 1958-59: Until Ben Lindsey's 1983 team, this was the year to forget in Arizona history. The UA went 4-22. Junior center Ernie McCray, the second African-American player at Arizona, was the marquee performer with a 15.9 scoring average and a 9.8 rebounding effort. McCray was a second-team Border player. He scored over 400 points and shot just over 40 percent from the field.

■ 1960-61: Joe Skaisgir came to Arizona on a basketball scholarship, but with more of an intent to excel in baseball. The Dearborn, Mich., native could not pass the opportunity to play hardball in the desert sun. First

Eli (Ted) Lazovich scored a Bear Down Gym-record 38 points in a 104-103 loss to Arizona State during the 1955 season. It was the first game Arizona ever scored over 100 points.

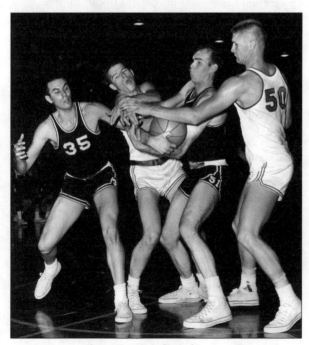

Joe Skaisgir's (second from left) hard-nosed persona typified the tough days of the Border Conference.

BILL REEVES

THE REBOUNDING MACHINE Don't look for tattoos all over Reeves' body, but the Arizona big guy had the same mentality as Chicago Bulls' bad boy Dennis Rodman.

"I won't say I have his off-the-court personality, but Rodman knows that he is limited at what he can do and makes the most of the things he does well," Reeves said. "That is what I tried to do. I didn't have a lot of ability. I was 6-4, probably 160 pounds. There was no such thing as a weight program, and I didn't know anything about fundamentals. I knew I could always rebound. There is a mentality if you know you can rebound you can help your team win games."

It helped that Reeves faced only two seven-footers during his career, but there is no ignoring his 13.2 rebounds as a junior and his 10.7 board per game average during his senior year.

"We had four shooters. They never got their hands dirty," Reeves said with a laugh. "They shot the ball and got the hell out of there. I'd go in and get the garbage and instead of laying it back up and in, like a stupid guy I would throw it back out to them so they could try again."

THE FOULING MACHINE On Reeves' desk is a small trophy, his "only memento from those days." The inscription isn't for leading the nation in points, or even rebounds — but for fouls.

"It was the only nice trophy I ever got," Reeves said. "I led the nation in average fouls per game in my senior year. That helps explain why my rebounds and points per game went down. I went from the MVP in my junior year to getting a trophy for the most fouls in my senior year. That was a thrill."

things first — basketball.

"I would miss about a month of baseball practice," Skaisgir said. "The guys would call me snowbird because when I came out of the field house I was as white as a ghost. They picked on me that first year, especially, until I got my bearings straight. It was good for me that I was a fast starter in the spring."

Skaisgir was a good finisher in basketball, becoming only the second Arizona player to score over 500 points in a season. Skaisgir also emerged as an all-American baseball player.

UDALLS GOVERN ARIZONA BASKETBALL COURTS

The Udall brothers — Mo and Stewart — from St. Johns, Ariz., made quite an impact on Arizona, and later, the country.

The two political activists excelled at the University of

Arizona by earning degrees and all-Border Conference honors.

Mo, who later became the first Wildcat ever to be drafted into the NBA, led the 1947-48 team in scoring with 13.2 points per game despite a glass eye — required after a childhood injury — that limited his depth perception.

Mo could see what the country needed. He endured a 30-year career as a representative of the second congressional district of Arizona and also ran for the Democratic presidential nomination against Jimmy Carter.

Stewart garnered all-league honors, but his best contribution to the basketball program was establishing a petition for the school to play better competition, which proved successful.

Stewart later served as the secretary of the Department of Interior under Presidents Kennedy and Johnson.

In 1966 the Udalls were honored by the NCAA for distinguishing themselves "academically and athletically during their undergraduate years."

In 1945 Stewart Udall showed his first sign of political leadership when he petitioned the Wildcats to schedule more difficult competition. His congressional career took off from there.

Mo Udall went from being the first Wildcat player ever drafted by the NBA to a 30-year career as a representative of the Second Congressional District of Arizona.

WAC(KY) Days With Larson

Recruiting, an outdated Bear Down Gym, political unrest, and participation in the much stronger Western Athletic Conference accounted for several of the problems facing Bruce Larson.

Bruce Larson was groomed to be Enke's replacement long before 1961. The nurturing process had begun more than a decade earlier.

From 1948 to 1950, Larson was a reserve for Enke's teams. At the start of the 1961 season, Larson replaced his mentor as the Wildcats' new head coach.

In Larson's 11 years of directing the school's basketball program, he faced changes in conferences, recruiting styles, and, most of all, the times.

Bear Down Gym, once a proud fixture in the Southwest, was considered an antique when Larson's tenure began. The days of roaming Texas in the Border Conference changed to the more demanding basketball played in the Western Athletic Conference. The recruiting budget at Arizona hardly was enough to drive past Phoenix.

Larson had several obstacles. Some of the biggest problems were those facing the nation. The civil-rights movement was going strong and the '60's flower child mentality was in full bloom.

"In those days the black revolution was going on. It was a period of demonstration," Larson said. "Players wanted to demonstrate. Bear Down was even set on fire before one game. The damage wasn't enough, so we still played. That was something you had to deal with. Nobody knew how because this was something new happening around the country.

"How do you let the blacks demonstrate or express themselves? Do they wear arm bands while they play? I think we allowed them. They also wanted to demonstrate at halftime, wanting to use the PA at halftime to express themselves. They wanted to use the game as a vehicle. People were experimenting on what we could do and not do."

Larson suited up four black starters. Teams in the WAC had substantial equity, as "UTEP's all-black starting lineup showed against all-white Kentucky" in the 1966 national championship game, Larson said.

Arizona also had an identity problem. Getting home-and-home series with some of the nation's best teams was impossible. Playing UCLA in Bear Down was unthinkable; yet the Wildcats played all the great Bruins teams in Los Angeles.

Larson's experience was limited on the major-college

level. After graduating from the UA in 1950, he coached Eastern Arizona for six years, which included a junior college national championship game. He also coached Weber Junior College (now Weber State) in Ogden, Utah, to back-to-back finals, winning the championship in 1959.

His success stemmed from defense. His wins at Arizona, which included many high-profile victories over top 20 teams, resulted from defense, which was consistently one of the best in the nation.

"Larson was a defensive wizard," said Warren Rustand, the best player of the Larson era. "We were always in the top 10. We were a nightmare for teams to play against us."

The Wildcats were quite formidable despite having to play almost every significant non-conference game on the road. Arizona struggled in WAC play.

"There were no pansies in the WAC," Rustand said.

Several times Arizona was regarded as the favorite to claim conference honors, but winning at Utah, BYU, and New Mexico proved too difficult. Larson wound up with a 136-148 record and recorded four winning seasons.

The odds were against him.

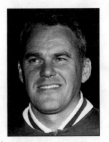

Bruce Larson played for the Wildcats in 1949 and 1950. After coaching stints at the junior college level, he took over the head coaching duties at Arizona in 1961.

1962-63: LIFE IN THE WAC

Surprising early season victories over top 10 teams gave the Wildcats a reason to be optimistic as they headed into their inaugural Western Athletic Conference campaign.

A 51-46 victory at Wisconsin and a 60-52 win over Colorado were signs that Larson's second team would end Arizona's six-year sub-.500 drought. The Wildcats wound up struggling against WAC foes, posting a 3-7 record for a fifth-place finish, and a 13-13 mark overall, the school's best win total since 1957.

Sophomores Albert Johnson and Rustand led the team in scoring and rebounding and were WAC all-second team selections. Johnson averaged 12.9 points and 9.7 rebounds, while Rustand averaged 10.6 points per game.

1963-64: OREO COOKIE EFFECT

Just like an Oreo cookie, the best part of the Wildcats' season was in the middle.

The Wildcats opened and closed the year with three straight defeats. Arizona posted victories over NIT finalist and WAC cochampion New Mexico, Pac-8 members California and USC, and Maryland and Evansville en route to winning the Evansville Christmas Tournament.

Following the 0-3 start, Arizona, again led by the duo of Johnson and Rustand, won 15 of 20 games. The 15-11 overall record was the school's first winning season in a decade. Five of those losses were by four points or less.

Rustand, a junior guard, was named a first-team all-WAC player despite Johnson leading the team in scoring (15.2) and rebounding (11). Johnson was named to the second-team.

1964-65: TOP TEAMS VICTIMIZED

Some way, somehow, the Wildcats continued to pull off upsets. The list of ranked victims during the Larson era grew.

Arizona sported a 17-9 record, the best mark in Larson's tenure. But the Wildcats were only 5-5 in league action. That meant little when playing the likes of No. 6 rated BYU, eighth-ranked San Francisco, and NIT-bound Bradley.

BYU fell, 75-73; San Francisco lost, 71-56; and Bradley ended up losing after three overtimes, 85-83. During one stretch, Arizona captured 10 of 11 victories. The win over San Francisco propelled the Wildcats into the national rankings for the first time since the 1950-51 season.

Larson's teams struggled, but Warren Rustand (1963-65) did not. He was a three-time all-WAC performer.

SENIORS GONE Rustand and Johnson played their last games as Wildcats. Rustand parlayed his 14.2 scoring average into first-team all-WAC honors and a position in the NABC East-West All-Star Game to become a fourth-round draft pick of the San Francisco Warriors.

Johnson concluded his career with 1,090 points and led the Wildcats in rebounding for the third straight year with nine per game. He had 775 boards during his career, which ranks seventh in school history.

1965-66: UPSETS GALORE

Plenty of extra playing time was granted to work on the transition from Johnson and Rustand to players like Ted Prickett, Bob Spahn, and Mike Aboud — including four overtimes during the course of the 15-11 season.

Three losses were the result, including an 81-72 defeat at Texas Western (now known as UTEP), the eventual NCAA champion. It took two extra periods for an 83-77 win over New Mexico.

NIT champ BYU (76-62) and Final Four participant Utah (71-68) both fell victim to the continual slate of impressive victories Larson posted against the "big

shots" of the college basketball scene.

Prickett, a 6-5 senior guard, was the top scorer at 16.5 points and second in rebounding at 7.2 as a second-team all-WAC player. Spahn's specialty was free-throw shooting. He converted on 85.9 percent of his attempts. Aboud was the top rebounder at 8.4.

1966-67: MISSING LINKS

With the top four scorers from the previous team gone, there was no way to prevent a down campaign. Bill Davis and Aboud did their best, but it was not enough as Arizona posted an 8-17 mark.

Davis, a 6-7, 180-pound forward, led the team in scoring with 15.4 points and in rebounding with 7.7, ranking in the top five in the WAC. Aboud, a 6-5 forward from Tucson, was second in rebounding with 6.1 boards per game.

1967-68: ELVIN HAYES DELIVERS

The first WAC championship at Arizona was expected to come this season. With Bill Davis returning, along with seven lettermen, the Wildcats were regarded as the class of the league.

So much for expectations. Arizona was 11-13 overall, 4-6 in conference action.

Davis did his share by earning first-team all-WAC honors with 17.5 points and 10.6 rebounds. He set single season and career records for field goal shooting with marksmanship of 51.4 and 49.1 percent, respectively.

TOO TOUGH A SCHEDULE Nine games were against ranked foes or those invited to play in postseason tournaments.

The most successful NCAA participant from the pictured 1965-66 team was not a player, but Arizona's freshman coach and Bruce Larson's varsity assistant — Cedric Dempsey, the current NCAA executive director (second from left standing).

AN NCAA EXECUTIVE DIRECTOR TO BE

Nobody had an inkling at the time, but Coach Bruce Larson's assistant (and Arizona's freshman coach) would become an Arizona athletic director and the current NCAA Executive Director.

Cedric Dempsey.

In September 1982, Dempsey — after AD stints at Pacific, Houston, and San Diego State — accepted the task of improving Arizona's financial state and reputation. Not only were dollars short, but tales were long of wrongdoing by the previous administration — and Dempsey had to deal with Ben Lindsey's disastrous 1982-83 basketball season.

Dempsey improved Arizona's facilities, put the program in the black, served on practically every NCAA committee imaginable, and in 1993 was named the executive director of the NCAA.

Former Arizona assistant basketball coach Cedric Dempsey pulled off a magical deed as the school's athletic director from 1982-93. He brought the school out of a budget crisis and aided in the establishing of several new athletic facilities, including the increased seating of McKale Center.

Losses to UTEP and Utah were both overtime affairs. The Wildcats did defeat New Mexico 69-68 as Mike Kordick scored a career-high 24 points.

ELVIN HAYES COMES TO TOWN Most trivia buffs remember the 1968 season because the Houston Cougars upset UCLA in the Astrodome during the regular season, ending the Bruins' 43-game winning streak. UCLA avenged the loss in the national championship game.

That same Houston team, with Elvin Hayes leading the Cougar charge, nearly found itself leaving Bear Down Gym on December 22 a loser, but the Cougars held off a rally to defeat Arizona, 81-76.

1968-69: GIANT IN THE MIDDLE

All was going well with 11 straight wins, but five consecutive losses down the stretch, including two one-point defeats to 17th-ranked Wyoming, cost Arizona the WAC title.

The Wildcats finished 17-10 overall and 5-5 in league

play. Five of the losses were by five points or fewer, and many of the defeats came to nationally ranked teams. In addition to Wyoming, Arizona fell victim to Seattle, 75-66; ninth-rated New Mexico State, 78-72; 12th-ranked Colorado, 70-69; and NCAA finalist Purdue, 98-72, at the Rainbow Classic in Hawaii.

SOPHOMORES Senior Jim Hansen, the lone starter from the year before, returned. Arizona took to the court with a sophomore-laden bunch, led by Mickey Foster (14.4 points), 6-5 Bill Warner (15.0), 6-8 Tom Lee (10.9), and 6-11 Eddie Myers (11.8). Each player scored in double figures.

STRETCH Myers emerged as the giant in Arizona basketball history — at least up to this point. The 6-11 center was the tallest player to don a Wildcat jersey. He took advantage of his height by leading the team and conference in rebounding with 10.3 boards per game, 11.2 in WAC play.

1970-72: FAVORITES FALTER

With the sophomores back, the Wildcats were favored to win their first WAC crown. It was not to be. A disappointing start to the season, with losses to defending national champion UCLA and Final Four participant New Mexico State, were too much to overcome as Arizona finished 12-14 overall, 8-6 in the WAC.

The Wildcats did make one final run despite the loss of Eddie Myers at the semester break. Arizona won 9 of 15 games, thanks largely to Warner, who averaged 20.3 points per game, 21.6 points in league action.

Warner amassed 38 points in an 80-78 victory over New Mexico and 31 points in a 90-89 win at Arizona State. He wound up being a second-team WAC player and was the third athlete in Arizona school history to record more than 500 points in a season, compiling 529 points.

Foster led the Wildcats in scoring with 12.4 points and shot a school record 85.5 percent from the free-throw line. Foster was among five players who scored in double figures: Warner (20.3), Foster (12.3), Tom Lee (11.9), Walt McKinney (10.2) and Myers (10.3).

The Wildcats were again tabbed as the team to beat in 1971. But Arizona did worse than the year before, finishing 10-16 and last in the WAC.

Arizona had four starters back, plus Eddie Myers. That lineup produced a 7-5 non-conference record, which included a Poinsettia Classic Championship in Greenville, S.C., with victories over Mississippi State and Texas A&M.

WILDCAT QUIZ

5. Who were the teams to to start and break Arizona's 81-game home court winning streak?

There was no stopping Bill Warner when he was "on." Warner was a true scorer, the school's first player to reach back-to-back 20-plus point seasons. He finished his career (1969-71) with 1,462 points and an 18.7 scoring average.

Three straight losses in league play ended any hope Larson had for claiming that elusive WAC title. He would conclude his coaching career the following season with a 6-20 mark.

Arizona did shape the conference race with an 82-77 victory over UTEP in the next to last game of the year. That prevented the Miners from sharing the league title with BYU. Warner scored 24, while Tom Lee put in 23 points and grabbed 15 rebounds.

WARNER'S WARNING Bill Warner, a 6-4 forward from Phoenix, was the first player in Arizona history to record back-to-back 20-plus point seasons. He averaged 20.9 as a senior.

Warner tallied 22.8 points in league play, including a 31-point, 14-rebound performance against BYU during an 81-76 victory. His 34-point outburst against Arizona State on February 20 in Bear Down Gym pushed him past Ernie McCray as the school's career scoring leader. Warner finished with 1,462 points and a career scoring clip of 18.7.

MATADOR DEFENSE This bunch of Wildcats in 1972 could score, recording 82.8 points per game, but the team's inability to stop the opposition became comical: its defense permitted a still-existing school-record 85.2 points per outing.

WILDCAT QUIZ

6. Who was the first African-American to play for the Wildcats?

Snow Job: Excitement Returns to UA Hoops

Fred "The Fox" Snowden is regarded as a pioneer, but without his wife, Maye, the legendary Detroit product never would have become a Wildcat.

Following the 1971 season then Arizona Athletic Director Dave Strack, a former Michigan Wolverine coach who had been acquainted with Snowden for years at Northwestern High School, knew who would be right to replace Bruce Larson on the bench.

Arizona was in desperate need of a basketball coach. Strack cared little that Snowden's skin was not white. At Strack's urging, Snowden came out for an interview but went home thinking his job as a Wolverine assistant coach to Johnny Orr was just fine.

Think again.

"(Maye) felt I had worked so hard that I should at least have the opportunity to make it," Snowden said in an article in the 1981-82 Arizona basketball program. "I

Fred Snowden became the second black major college coach in the country when he was hired prior to the 1972-73 season. Snowden brought excitement back to Arizona basketball following decades of disappointment. He recorded a mark of 167-108 in the process.

wasn't hung up about it, but in the end she was right."

It also did not hurt that Snowden could move away from the freezing weather.

"I recall the night Snowden came back to Detroit after interviewing for the job," said Larry Donald, publisher of *Basketball Times*. "We sat together at a Detroit Pistons game, and he was very uncertain whether or not to take the job because the Wildcat program had struggled for such a long time. As we left Cobo Arena in downtown Detroit and walked into the freezing winter night, I pointed out to Snowden that, at the very least, he wouldn't have to face these conditions in Tucson. We laughed."

Whether it was Maye's urging, the weather, or simply his time to follow a dream, Snowden accepted the head coaching job at Arizona.

"After the press conference in Tucson (announcing my hiring) I just sat down and cried," Snowden said. "I felt that being the first man of my race to become a head basketball coach at a major university was something to be proud of. And I was proud."

DISCRIMINATION FEARS "I don't think I am going to have to worry about whether I am the first black coach or the 40th. ... As far as recruiting, I don't recruit black

Contrary to popular belief, Coach Fred Snowden was not the first black head coach of a major university. Illinois State hired Will Robinson in 1970.

His flair, run-and-gun approach, and drive to achieve were non-stop.

McKale Center has grown to be one of the most feared arenas in college basketball. The fright started in Snowden's days and has picked up significantly since Lute Olson's arrival.

basketball players or white basketball players," Snowden was quoted in *The Arizona Daily Star*. "I recruit kids first and basketball players second."

Snowden was part of the first NCAA game featuring two black head coaches. Arizona defeated Georgetown, coached by John Thompson, 83-76 on March 13 in the first round of the 1976 NCAA tournament.

FIRST GAME-LAST GAME Snowden premiered the Kiddie Korps with a 94-87 victory over Cal-State Bakersfield.

"If Freddie had not done what he did, Lute would never have come here," former Snowden player Bob Elliott said. "There are a lot of programs around the country that have never had that fire. I know one of the attractive aspects of Arizona that brought Lute here was that he knew that a fire had been lit before. It was a matter of relighting it."

Ten years later the Snowden flame blew out, along with his basketball career, with a 96-78 win over Oregon in McKale Center. There were 11,529 fans in attendance. Greg Cook scored 28 and Frank Smith added 17 in the finale.

IMMEDIATE RESULTS During his first five years Snowden set the pace in the WAC. His 48-22 record in league play and a 102-39 overall mark was clearly above the rest. Wins in McKale Center were nearly a gimmee.

In that same five-year span, the Wildcats won 95 percent of their home games, including a streak of 38 straight from 1975-77. At one point, Arizona was 62-3.

THE FOX Many wonder how a man born in Brewton, Ala., on April 3, 1936, earned the nickname "The Fox." The answer: it came from his extraordinary base running ability.

At Northwestern High School Snowden earned all-conference honors as a basketball guard and a shortstop in baseball. After graduation, he attended Wayne State, where he majored in English and physical education and minored in speech and journalism.

Snowden hit .482 and had a reputation for Ozzie Smith-like skills on defense.

THE TEMPTATIONS After college, he returned to Northwestern High School as a varsity basketball and assistant baseball coach. Snowden worked with such future greats as standout first-baseman John Mayberry of Toronto, journeyman Willie Horton, American league batting champion Alex Johnson, and Olympic gold-medal winner Henry Carr (who won the 200 meter at the 1964 Games).

Two of his favorite athletes were Melvin Franklin and Richard Street, who would become members of the singing group The Temptations. (His secretary was Florence Ballard, a Supreme.)

"At Northwestern he had players that ended up with the Four Tops and the Temptations. If we ever showed up when they were around, (the groups) were there," Bob Elliott said. "So here we have the Temptations in our locker room before games. We would have the Four Tops right there with us.

"Obviously, we played a lot of Motown. On the stereo in the locker room if we tried to sneak a little George Clinton, Funky Delight, Freddie would come in there and turn that stuff off. You either had to listen to the Four Tops or the Temptations or a little Marvin Gaye. It all had to have some rhythm and tone to it. It couldn't be wild and crazy like George Clinton. The Four Tops and the Temptations were Freddie's Boys."

BY THE NUMBERS At Northwestern High School Snowden was 80-0 in five years as a JV basketball coach and 89-7 as a varsity coach for five years, including a 59-1 mark in conference play and five league championships.

He finished his Arizona career with a 167-108 record, a 28-44 mark in the Pac-10 and a 54-30 WAC record.

WILDCAT QUIZ

7. How did Fred Snowden earn his nickname "The Fox"?

Three 20-wins seasons, two trips to the NCAA tournament, including a contest against UCLA in the 1976 Western Regional Final, and an NIT berth were accomplished during his tenure.

CLOSING REMARKS Snowden won nearly 61 percent of his games at Arizona.

"I was 5-feet-8 1/2 and I wanted to be a basketball player," Snowden said. "There weren't many people encouraging that when I was growing up.

"I wanted to be a coach. There weren't very many people encouraging that, either, because there were no black coaches.

"They said you must be out of your mind. So I did the motivating myself. I've always believed that if you want something bad enough and work hard enough it will happen for you. ...

"I have somewhat mixed feelings, as coaching has been a major part of my life for the past 24 years. However, the opportunity to further my career and broaden my interests by going into administration is something I just can't pass up. It seems like just yesterday that I was starting. I've had a great career as a coach, and I have no regrets at all."

When Arizona historians think of point guards, Damon Stoudamire, Steve Kerr, and Russell Brown come to mind. But include Eric Money in that illustrious group.

FINAL DAYS After his basketball career, Snowden became the executive director of The Food 4 Less Foundation, which has received special citations from the Clinton Administration for its work with inner cities.

Snowden died on January 17, 1994, of cardiac arrest in Washington D.C. after a meeting with President Bill Clinton to determine better ways to improve inner cities.

Nearly 1,000 friends and family members appeared at a memorial in McKale Center for Snowden. Those in attendance included many of his former players, Tucson community leaders and peers.

Following Snowden's death, letters and cards were sent to Bob Elliott expressing their condolences, including messages from fellow black coaches George Raveling, John Thompson, Kelvin Sampson, and Rudy Washington.

"Every last one of them said the same thing," Elliott said. "If Freddie hadn't done what he did, people would have been hesitant to give us a chance to be a head coach."

1972-73: KIDDIE KORPS

With seven newcomers, five freshmen and a pair of junior college transfers, the Snowden era was ushered in with a group labeled "the Kiddie Korps." It would be Arizona's first taste of basketball glory on a national scale.

One could only imagine the entertainment value this team might have had with a shot clock, with a three-point line, and without the no-dunking rule. This was not a team known for its fundamentals — or its patience.

The first player to touch the ball usually took the shot. Plays. Yeah, right.

With the likes of Eric Money, Coniel Norman, Jim Rappis, Al Fleming, and John Irving the Wildcats raced to a 16-10 record, a 10-game improvement from the previous year.

MONEY IN THE BANK Few point guards in the country could distribute and shoot the ball like Eric Money, a freshman from Detroit's Kettering High School. Only Norman finished the WAC season with more points.

"Money was not your typical point guard who wanted to pass the ball all the time," said Bob Elliott, who would join the team a year later. "Money felt as long as the ball was in his hands he should make something happen. He believed in scoring 18 points and having 10 assists every game. He had his own philosophy of how to play. He felt if you back off of me, you are dead. If you guard me close, I will penetrate and score or dish off. He always kept everybody involved."

He also had a tendency to talk.

"Money was great in giving teams bulletin-board stuff.

Eric Money razzed opposing crowds, wore stylish outfits, and threw outlandish passes, but that never interfered with his ability to get the ball either to the open man or into the basket.

Nobody in the WAC could defend sharp-shooting Coniel Norman. His 576 points, 24-point average, and six school records were more than enough to earn him the WAC's Most Valuable Player award as a freshman. "Coniel Norman was the greatest shooter I ever played with in my life, ever, easily," Bob Elliott said.

We were at a game once — I don't remember where it was — but Money had made some statements. The place was wired up and crazy," Elliott said. "Eric didn't help the situation any. During warm-ups he would be yelling at the crowd as only Eric Money could do. He was the type of guy that would do that and then before the game started he would get us all together and say, 'All right I've blown my mouth off now. You all have to back me up.'"

Normally Money did not need much help as he averaged 18.9 points as a freshman.

WAC MVP Norman was no ordinary freshman. The former high school teammate of Money emerged as one of the premier players in the country with his extravagant scoring ways.

No. 22 had several 40-point games without the three-point shot. He set a UA single-season record with 576 points, a 24-point per game average, and led the WAC in scoring.

Norman was also the WAC's Most Valuable Player and made several national all-freshman teams. In the process he broke or tied six Arizona scoring records and the WAC record for field goals (242) in a season.

"Coniel Norman was the greatest shooter I ever played with in my life, ever, easily," Bob Elliott said. "As a kid you play a game called 21. You have to score and then you get a chance to go to the free throw line. Norman would go to the top of the key and knock down 19 in a row and the game was over. We would throw the ball at his feet, at head, make him turn around, anything to distract him, but it didn't make any difference."

KIDDIE KORPS There has been a lot of talk about the No. 1 rated recruiting class that Lute Olson signed in 1996, but Mike Bibby, Stephen Jackson, Eugene Edgerson, and Bennett Davison have a long way to go to equal the first-year exploits of the Kiddie Korps.

The Kiddie Korp combined to score 1,578 points. The Sean Elliott/Anthony Cook/Kenny Lofton class registered 811 points, while Bob Elliott, Herman Harris and Jerome Gladney scored 657. Joseph Blair, Corey Williams and the Reggie Geary freshman group managed 462.

Just how good this class could have been never was seen. Money and Norman filed for hardship into the NBA after their sophomore years, while Rappis was continually hampered by ankle and back problems, and Irving eventually transferred to Hofstra, where he led the country in rebounding during the 1975 season.

McKALE CENTER OPENING The first seven home games of the season were in Bear Down Gym, all victories. On

The Wildcats played the first seven home games of Fred Snowden's tenure in Bear Down Gym, but by 1973 McKale Center was up and operating. Pictured are Snowden and then Arizona Athletic Director Dave Strack in front of the construction of McKale Center.

February 1, 1973, the Wildcats debuted McKale Center. An overflow crowd of 13,652 watched Arizona defeat Wyoming, 87-69. Norman scored a game-high 37 points.

McKale consisted of a state-of-the-art athletic facility, that included 46 offices, five handball courts, three classrooms, storage rooms for the drama department, whirlpools, examination rooms, exercise rooms, and two large scoreboards that not only showed time and score, but player and team fouls, time-outs, and wrestling rounds. (That was a big deal back then).

The structure was proposed in 1967, but it took three years to gather the money. Then two years of construction increased the original estimate of $2 million to $8.4.

1973-74: BOMBS AWAY

Arizona's season-opening 101-80 victory over Illinois was no fluke — these Wildcats were going to score some points.

Lots and lots of them:

Arizona 101	Illinois 80	
Arizona 109	San Diego State 79	
Arizona 101	Idaho 80	
Utah 121	Arizona 106	
Arizona 118	BYU 90	
Arizona 122	Utah 92	

Arizona scored in the 90s in seven other games. When the year was complete, the Wildcats had averaged a school-record 89 points and set a standard with a 50.2 field goal percentage.

Norman led the WAC in scoring with 23.8 points

Al Fleming led the team in rebounding in 1973 with 9.9 boards per game and in 1975 with 11.8 an outing.

Al Fleming (54) was not one of the more noticeable members of the Kiddie Korps, but his rebounds were essential and his presence a necessity as he became the WAC's best player in 1976.

overall, 25.5 points in league action. Al Fleming was deadly inside with a nation-leading 66.7 percent field goal mark. Arizona finished the year 19-7 and in second place in the WAC.

FLEMING FLAIR Norman and Money were outgoing, Elliott had a charisma about him, and Snowden always drew a crowd. Lost in the shuffle was the shy, quiet Fleming, Arizona's power forward.

"I don't think he has gotten the kind of credit he deserves," Elliott said. "Some of that is because of the people that he played with. He came in with the Kiddie Korps. Eric Money is a very vivacious personality. People tended to drift to him. Al is an unassuming type of guy who got lost in the shuffle. But when the game was over he had 12 rebounds, 15 points and he shot 6-of-8 from the field. He was a very steady person. He got the job done."

ROUTE 66, I-94 BETTER Arizona's emergence was credited to Snowden's knowledge and recruiting ability along Interstate 94 in the Michigan, Indiana, and Wisconsin area.

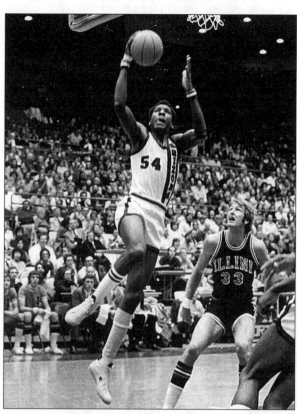

Coniel Norman (22) was more a shooter than a rebounder during his two-year Wildcat career. He left early for the NBA.

"Freddie literally caught a plane to Detroit, got on I-94, picked up Money, Norman, and (Jerome) Gladney out of Detroit," Bob Elliott recalled. "And then he moved about 20 miles, went north for about 10 miles to pick up Timmy Marshall out of Pontiac Central (High School), went a little further to the north and picked up Greg Lloyd from Lansing, Michigan. He then flew back down to get me out of Ann Arbor, Michigan, then tried to pick up Tony Dungy out of Jackson. We knew each other since kids. We said we were a package deal.

"Fred goes all the way to Michigan City, Indiana, still on I-94 to pick up Al Fleming and then to Gary, Indiana, to pick up Larry Demic and then he flew to Chicago to pick up Sylvester Maxey, as well as Bob Aleksa. I-94 curls around the lake into Wisconsin where he finds Jim Rappis. It was the I-94 recruiting trip. The budget had to look pretty great."

THE MICHIGAN CONNECTION Long before all the Detroit products had relocated to Tucson, Snowden, Norman,

Money, Elliott, et al knew each another. They were already like one big happy basketball family.

"Eric (Money) and I played together on a team in high school that represented the city of Detroit," Bob Elliott said. "Part of the reason Freddie ended up with Coniel, Eric, Gladney, and myself is because we were all on the same team. We were in a national tournament representing Detroit. We won the tournament.

"We beat in the finals a team from Washington D.C., which had Adrian Dantley and Moses Malone playing on it. Afterwards we were sitting there saying, 'Let's take this act some place else together.' We all agreed we wanted to stick together."

They did.

Elliott and Money became almost inseparable. Not only did Elliott have to lie to play in that nationally sponsored tournament — by using Money's address as his home — the two would later go on to play pro basketball together in New Jersey.

"I don't know how many people can say they played with somebody in high school, college, and the pros together," Bob Elliott said.

As for the connection between Elliott and Snowden, they knew each other for years, since both lived in Ann Arbor.

"He was an icon to me," Elliott said. "I had known him since I was 12 years old when he was an assistant at Michigan. By the time he took the job here he was paving a path for other people to follow."

WILDCAT QUIZ

8. Instead of Ben Lindsey, who was the key guy offered the job first?

1974-75: MONOPOLY ANYBODY

Snowden was facing a year of transition — in so many ways.

After a great deal of success by playing a high standard of pickup basketball, the Wildcats were forced to utilize a slow down, methodical approach with Bob Elliott and Al Fleming inside.

"Utah's Jerry Pimm called us the Monopoly offense: Put Boardwalk and Park Place down low and build the hotels on them and forget the rest of them," Bob Elliott said.

Boardwalk had Fleming firmly entrenched, while Elliott called Park Place home.

Then Money and Norman both declared for the NBA draft, and Snowden had to feel like he picked up a "go directly to jail" card.

That was only the start of change. Ronald Allen and James Wakefield both graduated, and Arizona's leftover guard combination of Gilbert Myles and Rappis were both ailing. Myles nursed torn cartilage in his knee and Rappis had an ankle that needed surgery. Both had to wait until the season was complete.

Instead of trying to score 100 points, the Wildcats used a deliberate pace.

"To walk the ball up the floor might have been a medical decision more than a talent decision," Bob Elliott said. "If your point guard and your off guard both need surgery, what are you going to do?"

CHANGE IS GOOD Despite the completely new philosophy, Arizona finished the year 22-7 and runner-up in the National Commissioners Invitational in Louisville, Ky.

The Wildcats, in the school's first postseason competition in 25 years, defeated East Carolina, 94-78, and then Purdue, 102-96, before losing to Drake, 83-76, in the championship game.

1975-76: UCLA PREVENTS FINAL FOUR

Some would say the best team in Arizona history was the unit that suited up against UCLA in Pauley Pavilion in the West Regional Championship of the NCAA Tournament.

The Wildcats had virtually everything a team needed — plenty of perimeter scoring with Herm "The Germ" Harris and Jim Rappis, and an over-abundance of inside power with Phil Taylor, Elliott, and Fleming owning the paint. But as good as it was, this squad might have been better with Norman and Money — both would have been seniors.

That 24-9 season included the school's first WAC title, a near berth in the Final Four, and some historical significance.

McKALE RECORD With minutes remaining and a victory over Detroit in hand, Snowden had the luxury of benching Fleming, who had 33 points at halftime and 37 when he was taken out.

Fleming had toweled off and leaned back in his chair when Snowden was informed four points were needed to set a McKale Center record. In went Fleming. Out went the old record. Fleming's 41-point performance still stands as the UA's home scoring mark to beat.

Herman Harris was instrumental in Arizona's appearance in the 1976 NCAA Western Regional finals against UCLA in Pauley Pavilion. His scoring insured a 114-109 victory over UNLV two days earlier. Harris scored 16 of the team's final 27 points in regulation against the high-flying Rebels. "The Germ's" presence was not enough in an 82-66 loss to the Bruins.

An ankle injury prevented starting guard Jim Rappis from playing at full-strength late in his Arizona career, but his leadership and outside shooting spearheaded the Wildcats to national prominence.

Fleming's line overshadowed Bob Elliott, who had 30 points and 10 rebounds.

WAC TITLE For years Arizona had been the whipping boy for the Sun Devils of Arizona State. But with a 77-72 victory in front of 14,618 fans at McKale Center, the Wildcats clinched their initial WAC title and the school's first league crown since the 1951 Border championship.

Arizona took a commanding 11-2 lead. Bob Elliott handled the Sun Devils the rest of the way with 21 points and 11 boards.

Fleming was the force throughout the season as he was named the WAC's MVP, earning six of eight first-place votes from the coaches. The Wildcat center also became the conference's rebounding leader and the top player in the USBWA.

ODDS AGAINST Heading into the NCAA tournament, Indiana, with its undefeated regular season record, was the favorite to win the NCAA championship with 2-to-1 odds. UCLA was 4-to-1, with UNLV 8-to-1. Arizona was a 20-to-1 long shot to win the crown.

HOLLERIN' HOYAS From a sociological standpoint, Arizona's 83-76 victory over Georgetown in the ASU Activity Center in Tempe was truly significant: the first matchup of black head coaches. From a basketball perspective, it marked the first NCAA Tournament win in school history.

All five Arizona starters scored in double figures. Rappis led the way with 20. Taylor added 15, Elliott 14, Harris 13, and Fleming 12. The Wildcats built an 18-point lead in the first half and then hung on in the final minutes.

RUNNIN' WITH THE REBELS Pepperdine's Gary Colson warned the Wildcats that running with the Rebels would be wrong.

"If Arizona tries to go up and down the court they'll score a lot of points, but Vegas will win," Colson said.

The Pepperdine coach had the right to spout off after giving UNLV its only loss in 30 regular season games, but Arizona was not about to change. During a 98-94 loss earlier in the season at Las Vegas, the Wildcats had managed to give the Rebels all they could handle, cutting a 15-point deficit to four.

Arizona felt confident it had the horses to run — and win.

This was the first UNLV team to master the run-and-gun approach. The Rebels entered the NCAA tournament with a 110-point scoring clip.

Portland State, with 115 points, thought it had the offense. UNLV won by 15. NAU scored 101 and lost by 38. Hawaii-Hilo scored 111 and lost by 52. UNLV's 163-111 victory over Hawaii-Hilo set an NCAA record for points scored.

Herman Harris was not fazed by UNLV; he scored 31 points, including 16 of the team's last 27 points in regulation to send the game into overtime. Harris had to continue his magic as Rappis and Fleming both fouled out.

The Wildcats went toe to toe with UNLV, with most of the jabs coming from the free throw line. In overtime Arizona made 11-of-14 attempts to pull the upset of the tournament, winning 114-109. The Wildcats did not convert a field goal in the extra period.

WOODEN GONE-BRUINS BACK John Wooden's retirement a year earlier had many fans in Westwood upset, especially after they were forced to endure a 25-4 season! Gene Bartow had the burden of replacing UCLA's legendary coach. Arizona had the unenviable

WILDCAT QUIZ

9. Can you name the four victories Lindsey compiled during the 1982-83 season?

task of playing the Bruins in Pauley Pavilion in the NCAA Western Regional finals.

Over the previous 10 years, UCLA had lost three times at home. But this year there was no Alcindor or Walton present. This Bruin team was made up of Richard Washington, David Greenwood, Marques Johnson, and Roy Townsend.

Two days earlier the Wildcats had been extended against UNLV. Rappis walked around the team's hotel on the day of the UCLA game on crutches. Everything marked doom for Arizona.

The Wildcats managed to stay within three at halftime, but a 12-point run midway through the second half was too much to overcome in Arizona's 82-66 loss.

CONSEQUENCES A large welcoming party met the team at the airport that night to say "thanks for the memory."

As for Snowden, he was a hot coaching commodity. Wisconsin and Michigan State were knocking on his door, job openings in hand.

1977-82: TURBULENT TIMES

Bob "Big Bird" Elliott became the school's all-time leading scorer until Sean Elliott eclipsed his mark more than a decade later. Bob Elliott concluded his career with 2,131 points, an 18.7 per game average.

Expectations had been raised to unseen heights. That produced the challenge of having to exceed the preceding year's accomplishments. With nearly everybody coming back, the last thing anybody thought possible was an opening-round NCAA Tournament loss.

But that is exactly what happened, as Southern Illinois defeated Arizona, 81-77, ending the Wildcats' 1977 season with a 21-6 record. It was the first time in school history the program had three consecutive 20-plus win seasons.

BIG BIRD FLEW AWAY Bob "Big Bird" Elliott concluded his career as the school's all-time leading scorer with 2,131 points. Only Sean Elliott has managed to pass the popular Wildcat big man.

CATCH THIS There were few anywhere who were better at getting the ball to the right man at the right place at the right time than Russell Brown. His numbers are amazing.

From 1978-81, Brown amassed 810 assists — 147 more than Damon Stoudamire — who occupies second place in the Arizona record books. Stoudamire was good, and Steve Kerr is regarded as one of the school's top point guards, but Brown might have been the best.

"He was the best passer ever," teammate Joe Nehls

said. "When people list the best point guards, they forget to mention Russell Brown, which is unbelievable. Kerr can shoot the ball and Stoudamire had the range and the quickness, but Russell Brown was like a little of them both."

Brown averaged 7.6, 9.1, 7.4, and 6.1 assists on four mediocre teams. He still owns the McKale record with 19 assists against Grand Canyon in 1979. In fact, five of the top single-game assist records have Brown's signature by them, as do nine of the top 13 assist games in school history.

SCORING DEMIC Larry Demic excelled during Snowden's later years, averaging 19.3 points as a senior, but more importantly for the Wildcats he controlled the paint.

Russell Brown (10) would get the ball to the right man at the right time. His 810 career assists may never be equaled. Brown (1978-81), who has 147 more assists than No. 2 Wildcat Damon Stoudamire, averaged 7.9, 9.1, 7.4 and 6.1 assists with four very average teams. He had a school record 19 assists against Grand Canyon and owns 9 of the school's top 13 game records.

Larry Demic (with block) was one of the few bright spots late in Snowden's career. The Wildcat center's 20 points and eight rebounds was crucial in Arizona's 70-69 victory over highly-regarded UCLA in 1979. Demic averaged 19.3 points and 10.3 rebounds as a senior.

The most exciting two-game series in Snowden's final six years came early in the 1979 season with back-to-back upsets of UCLA (70-69) and USC (74-72) at home.

Demic had 7.8 rebounds per game in 1978 and 10.3 a year later to earn all-Pac-10 honors. He played his best against the Bruins during the 1978-79 season, scoring 20 points and grabbing eight rebounds in a 70-69 victory on Jan. 18, 1979 and scoring 38 points with nine rebounds in a loss Feb. 17.

TOUGH TIMES FOLLOWED The first-round loss was a prelude of difficult times for the Arizona basketball program. Except for a weekend sweep of USC and highly-touted UCLA during the 1979 season, the Wildcat basketball team had to live off past successes.

From 1977 to 1982 Arizona posted a 65-69 record, played no NCAA tournament games, and failed to place higher than fourth in WAC or Pac-10 play. (The Wildcats joined the Pac-10 on July 1, 1978.)

PAC-10 EMERGENCE The Pacific schools wanted Arizona State as an addition to their already powerful base and accepted Arizona in their expansion.

But the Wildcats didn't manage to recruit as well after joining the league. Snowden's once powerful Midwestern base had disappeared, and Arizona's clout in the West

Years later in alumni all-star games, Bob Elliott returned to take on stars from different eras.

Had there been a three-point shot, Joe Nehls might have bested Steve Kerr as Arizona's all-time outside shooter. Nehls' patented jump shot was deadly. He made 50.8 percent of his attempts in 1978, mostly from 20-feet and way beyond.

was non-existent.

"Hindsight is 20-20," Bob Elliott said. "I think Freddie felt if the UCLA programs can be built on the LA kids, so could his. Arizona had just moved to the Pac-10 at that time. He felt like he could fight fire with fire."

ACCUSATIONS In the waning years of Snowden's tenure, "The Fox" faced alleged slush fund stories and accusations, the transfers of several players, numerous academic probations, the turnover of his coaching staff, and a decline in attendance and interest in Wildcat basketball.

In a two-year span attendance dropped in McKale

BOMB SCARE

Despite the insistence by WAC officials Larry Stubing and Stan Watts, the February 18, 1977, Arizona game against Utah was called off with 45 seconds left.

"There was a bomb threat," Bob Elliott recalled. "Jeff Jonas was a point guard with Utah. He came up to me and said, 'Do you believe some fool really tried to call in a bomb threat?' Hey, you have to deal with reality. Reality was a minute and a half left in the game, there is a dead ball and the announcer comes over the PA and says, 'Ladies and gentlemen, at the conclusion of this game please file out as soon as possible. A bomb threat has been called into the arena.'

"I'm looking at Freddie saying, 'Fred, let's get the 'F' out of here.' Fred says there is only a minute and something left. I said what

good is that if this thing actually happens. I'm not willing to sit here and play another minute, if in fact this is not a hoax. It is not about all of this. We've been called the 'N' word all over the places that we've played. We have been pelted with apples and oranges and cans before. All it takes is one lunatic. I told Fred, 'You can stay and play if you want to, but I'm out of here.' Everybody else is like, 'We are with Bird.' We said this one is over, take the W."

Utah was clearly going to win anyway, up by 15, but still the WAC officials tried to keep Arizona's staff on the court.

The team put street clothes over its jerseys and left. After some thoughts of declaring the game a forfeit, it went down as a 76-61 loss. No bomb was ever found.

Center by nearly 2,500. Fans came to games with paper bags over their heads with "MildCats" and "Who U" written on them.

Nobody could possibly have imagined Arizona's fate would get even worse following Snowden's resignation in 1982.

1982-83:
Lindsey's Lone Stand

Arizona basketball Coach Jim Harrick.

That was one of many possibilities following the resignation of Fred Snowden. Others were Tennessee's Don DeVoe, Fresno State's Boyd Grant, Wyoming's Jim Brandenburg, Illinois State's Bob Donewald, former Detroit Piston and Tucson gunner Herb Brown, Idaho's Don Monson, and Kansas State's Jack Hartman.

Ben Lindsey's one year was tumultuous at best. His 4-24 campaign included allegations of wrongdoing, player revolt, and coaching misdirection.

Those were the realistic choices, although the Arizona athletic director still had hopes of hiring somebody like Bobby Knight or Lute Olson.

Lute said "no" right after the conversation reached "hello." Knight never considered the job seriously.

That left Hartman as the main candidate. The Kansas State coach looked over the position, examined his options and said as the others: "Thanks, but no thanks." In fact, Hartman declined twice.

"Strack went from wanting Bobby Knight to Ben Lindsey," said former player and heavily involved alum Bob Mueller with chagrin.

Lindsey was hired March 31, 1982. It was an early April Fool's joke. Lindsey's team was constantly in turmoil, to the point of player revolts. He lost a school-record 24 games, defeated only Stanford in Pac-10 action, and helped cause a serious decay in basketball excitement in Tucson.

But none of this could be foreseen at the time the job was offered. Lindsey had excellent credentials at the NAIA level, guiding Grand Canyon College to two national championships, while compiling a 317-137 record in 16 years.

PHIL SLAMMA JAMMA The Houston Cougars advanced to the NCAA championship game before being upset by North Carolina State. Despite the setback, many consider Guy Lewis' team one of the best in Division I history. Arizona discovered this the hard way in the season opener, losing 104-63.

"I've taken beatings, but I was embarrassed as a coach," Lindsey told *The Arizona Daily Star*. "We were doing stuff I couldn't believe."

The Cougars' duo of Akeem Olajuwon and Clyde Drexler were simply too much for the undersized, talent-bereft Wildcats. If Houston needed added motivation, the victory was the 500th of Lewis' career.

"I didn't think he was going after his 500th," Lindsey said. "I think he was going for 500 points."

Houston opened with a 15-4 lead and was in front 53-26 by halftime. Arizona committed 33 turnovers, 21 in the first half.

THERE WERE SOME WINS Florida International became Lindsey's first victim as Arizona recorded a 79-68 victory in McKale Center. The Wildcats even managed a two-game winning streak, defeating Northern Arizona 66-53 and 19th-ranked San Diego State 46-44. That's when trouble came. It would be another 15 games before the next W would be recorded.

SIGNS OF DECAY Lindsey realistically had little time to recruit after his hiring. He also had to deal with the negligible talent Snowden left on the roster. It was a matter of time before the wheels fell off.

Here are some highlights of the team's turmoil:
■ KGUN-TV canceled Lindsey's coach's show.
■ *The Arizona Daily Star* polled the Wildcat players; five (anonymously) said Lindsey should be fired. "He's not ready for big time basketball," one player was quoted as saying.
■ Jack Magno was kicked off the team following an argument with Lindsey on January 14.
■ On January 22 several players set up a meeting with first-year Athletic Director Cedric Dempsey to discuss problems.
■ Todd Porter and David Haskins were benched for missing bed check before the game at USC.
■ Several players had to repay long-distance phone bills incurred at USC's press row the day before a game.
■ To save money the team flew into Los Angeles the day of a game and then sat around the team's hotel lobby until their rooms were available.
■ Two weeks into the season a "new offense" was installed during a two-hour practice.

Keith Jackson and several others continually put up with sporadic coaching philosophies, travel foul-ups, and losses — plenty and plenty of losses.

GIVE ME A BREAK Prior to a March 3 home game against Stanford, Lindsey called a news conference to discuss rumors and media reports that he would be fired. Lindsey neglected to inform the Arizona administration, notably Dempsey, of the gathering.

"As for myself and my future here at the UA, I made a commitment when I accepted this position that — given a reasonable amount of time — I would give the UA a program of championship caliber and one they would be proud of. And that if I failed to do so I would willingly step aside and give the next fellow his chance. I have not wavered from this commitment.

"I am personally confident that the program will soon show marked improvement. However, the job cannot be done overnight, certainly not by a coach who was hired at the 11th hour."

DISASTROUS ROAD LED TO NCAA TOURNAMENT

From Fred Snowden to Ben Lindsey to Lute Olson.

Brock Brunkhorst best understood the state of Arizona basketball prior to Lute Olson's arrival.

The 6-2 shooting guard from East Phoenix (Ariz.) High School had the distinction, or misfortune, of playing under three coaches during his four year Wildcat career.

Brunkhorst went through Snowden's swan song and finished with an NCAA tournament appearance. It was a whirlwind experience.

Under Snowden the program was at a standstill. Recruiting efforts had been limited and success was at an all-time low (or so people said).

"I think Coach Snowden knew he was on his way out," Brunkhorst said recently from his home in Phoenix. "He knew during the year he was going to leave. He probably didn't coach us as hard as the other teams. The cupboard was pretty bare."

Snowden's burnout was apparent, but his motivational skills remained keen.

"He could get you to do things. He could relate with everybody," Brunkhorst said. "Here I was, this skinny white kid, but he treated me like a black kid from wherever. Everybody was equal."

Unfortunately for Wildcat basketball the talent level between Arizona and the other Pac-10 teams was anything but equitable.

Brunkhorst and the gang concluded the 1981-82 season with a 9-18 record.

The change to Lindsey was accompanied by high hopes. That is, until reality set in.

Lindsey was not on the same playbook with the starting unit.

"I don't have too many nice things to say about that time," Brunkhorst said. "It was a bad situation for everybody. He was in way over his head. That was proven. I personally didn't get along with him or what he did with the program. It was a real disaster when we had Lindsey there."

For example:

■ "We never looked at game film. When Coach Olson came in he asked to see the films. It was like, 'What films?' We didn't even have a VCR."

■ "We opened the season with no break-the-press offense. A couple of the players came up to him and asked about it. He said, 'Just wait, we will figure that out when the game comes.' "

■ "I will never forget it, we were at Washington State, Lindsey got the team together and said, 'Don't embarrass yourselves tonight.' That was his pregame speech, telling us not to embarrass ourselves."

Two years later Brunkhorst was a starter in an NCAA Tournament game against Alabama.

Before that game the Wildcats went through what seemed like endless practices, growing pains and plenty of hard luck defeats.

"It makes you appreciate Lute's

LONE PAC-10 VICTORY In front of 5,711 fans, the smallest crowd ever in McKale Center, the Wildcats snapped their 15-game losing streak and recorded the team's only Pac-10 win of the season with a 74-73 triumph over

qualities a bit more, when at the time I thought he was really being too hard on us," Brunkhorst said.

"Now I realize he was just trying to make us better players and trying to turn the program around."

Guard Brock Brunkhorst (10) was ready to transfer before Ben Lindsey was fired after the 1982-83 season.

Stanford.

Morgan Taylor converted the front end of a one-and-one free throw with 13 seconds left to pull out the victory. While this Wildcat team did go on to record the worst record in school history, the longest losing streak was avoided.

The 1958-59 team had lost 16 straight games.

UA FIRES LINDSEY

–The Arizona Daily Star, March 16, 1983

After months of speculation the Wildcat administration pulled the trigger and fired Lindsey after his 4-24 season.

"In my best personal judgment Coach Ben Lindsey will be unable to overcome the conditions surrounding the program," Dempsey said at the news conference where he officially announced Lindsey's dismissal. He said the university would attempt "to locate a coach who will bring stability, long-range continuity, and success to the UA basketball program."

Lindsey was offered a year's severance pay of $49,000. That was not enough to buy Lindsey's silence.

"I do feel used. I feel my career has been damaged considerably," Lindsey told *The Arizona Daily Star*.

WILDCAT QUIZ

10. Who were the starters in Olson's first coached game against Northern Arizona in 1983?

LINDSEY (IN) COURT, NOT (ON) IT Lindsey sued the UA, saying he had been given a four-year "verbal" contract by former Arizona Athletic Director Dave Strack. (At that time Arizona universities were permitted to give only one-year contracts.)

Of Lindsey's $3.5 million lawsuit against the UA he was awarded $215,000 for lost salary and $480,000 for "career damage" in a jury trial. His attorney then asked for another $300,000, including $200,000 for interest and $100,000 for legal fees.

Pima County Superior Court Judge Lawrence Fleischman awarded $91,312 in attorney fees and $215,000 in interest, but during the appeals process Lindsey wound up losing again.

In December 1987, the appellate court declared the jury should not have awarded the $480,000 and that too much interest had been tabulated. On June 7, 1988, two months after Arizona had gone to the Final Four under Lute Olson, the Arizona Supreme Court denied a petition to review the case. After years of legal battles, Lindsey would receive the $215,000 originally given for lost salary.

SUPPORT GIVEN TO LINDSEY Few showed up for Wildcat games, but following Lindsey's firing support flowed in for the released coach.

Sam Pollack, *The Arizona Daily Star* sports editor, wrote "decency was apparently very low on the UA's list of priorities when it came to Lindsey."

Letters to the editor were printed for a couple of weeks, with the majority condemning Dempsey and the UA. On March 20, 10 letters were printed, all favoring Lindsey. Writers described the firing as "Disgraceful behavior." "A Rotten deal." "A mistake." "More changes needed (meaning Dempsey should be fired next)." "The structure stinks."

ASK AND DEMPSEY DELIVERED Following Lindsey's dismissal, Dempsey described the type of coach Arizona would seek:

"We expect the successful candidate to be a good recruiter, teacher, motivator and organizer. To be successful a candidate must have demonstrated integrity, reliability and concern for the student athletes in intercollegiate athletics."

On came Lute Olson.

Perfectionist Extraordinaire:
Lute Olson

The farm boy from North Dakota has always striven for perfection.

With every I dotted and every T crossed, Lute — as he is affectionately known — has reached precision because of a great eye for details and for his ability to communicate with young people.

He has been successful for more than 23 years in college and nearly 40 years of coaching in all.

Few have earned a reputation for turning bad

People thought Lute Olson had lost his mind when he left Iowa for a down-trodden Arizona program.

programs into national powerhouses, but Olson and his assistants have done it — twice.

In 1974, after one successful season at Long Beach State, Olson was hired to rebuild an Iowa program in desperate need. Taking one step at a time, Olson carried a last place team into the NCAA tournament in five years, and later into the Final Four.

The job done at Arizona is even more remarkable considering the depths to which the program sunk. By the conclusion of the 1982-83 season the Wildcats hit bottom, posting a 4-24 record, the worst mark in school history. Under Ben Lindsey Arizona was 1-17 in Pac-10 action.

At Iowa, Olson had become an icon. Everywhere he went, every time he turned around, somebody was staring, pointing fingers or asking for an autograph. Privacy — there was none.

Results — there were plenty.

The constant fishbowl in Iowa City became a little much. The attention, combined with the desire to go West, lured Olson to Tucson after Lindsey's dismissal.

People thought "the old guy had lost his wheels," Olson said.

As it turned out for Lute, his wife, Bobbi, and their five children, the move was right for everyone — especially Wildcat basketball fans.

Lute Olson has guided Arizona to 12 straight NCAA tournaments and posted a 316-101 record for the Wildcats.

LUTE AS A BOY Robert Luther Olson grew up in Mayville, N.D., a town with a population of 1,800. It was far removed from luxurious lifestyle he enjoys in Tucson now. Instead, he learned the harsh realities of a meager existence.

When Olson was 5 years old, his father passed away from a stroke. Nine months later his 21-year old brother, who had come home to run the family's farm, died in a tractor accident. That left his mom, who had a limited educational background, alone to support two teenagers.

To help out, Lute knocked on doors, asking to shovel snow or to mow lawns. By the sixth grade he became a flagger for crop-dusting planes dispensing DDT. At 11 Lute was driving without a license to transport his blind grandfather.

"I just propped myself on some pillows so I could see," Lute told the *San Francisco Chronicle*.

A YEAR EARLIER The UA administration tried to contact Olson before hiring Lindsey — Lute never even considered the opening.

"No, I didn't have an interest," Olson said. "We had raised all the money for the new arena in Iowa and had yet to play in there. I did not feel the timing was right.

Arizona contacted Bump Elliott, the AD, to get permission to talk to me. I indicated I couldn't in good conscience leave prior to the year we would be in Carver-Hawkeye Arena to play."

Olson didn't expect a second chance for the Arizona job considering Fred Enke's 36-year tenure, Bruce Larson's 11-year stint, and Fred Snowden's decade of work. History changed suddenly.

"I felt after declining to talk with them, 'Well, that is probably the end of that situation,'" Olson thought. "Usually, when you hire a coach there won't be a change until much further down the line. It was not a job that opened very often."

ONE-YEAR CONTRACTS "I'm not at all worried about a one-year contract. That is why I have this twitch in my right eye," Olson said with a laugh at the news conference to announce his hiring.

"I've never been one to be concerned about the length of contracts. I always felt if you didn't warrant to be employed, then you shouldn't be. I felt comfortable here, given the chance. At Iowa, in essence, I had almost a lifetime contract. It was a matter of how many years I wanted to be there. It was like a 10-year contract at that time. It could have been 20 if I wanted."

TOP TO THE BOTTOM There was no sound basketball reason to leave Iowa, if immediate results were being considered.

"In retrospect, you can wonder if it was the right move," Olson said. "The team at Iowa we had coming back was ranked No. 5 nationally in the preseason polls. The strength of that program was in its juniors. You knew one year it would be in the top five and the other it would be top five or better."

The Wildcats were viewed as one of the worst programs in the country.

WILDCAT QUIZ

11. What former Arizona coach played "Tarzan"?

"To come down here with a one-year contract and the program in very bad condition … it probably wasn't a very smart move," Olson said. "A lot of coaches I saw during that summer recruiting were wondering if I was nuts."

COACH OF THE YEAR After winning the Big Ten Coach of the Year award in 1979 and 1981 Olson started claiming similar accolades in the Pac-10, with honors arriving in 1986, 1988, 1989, 1993, and 1994.

Along with the conference honors, Olson was the national Coach of the Year at Arizona in 1988 and the CBS Coach of the Year in 1989.

The real coach in the Olson clan might be Bobbi, Lute's wife.

ALOOF Many believe Olson stands above everybody else and looks down on some. Those who have gotten to know the white-haired coach have a different outlook.

"He has gotten a bad rap for being too tight, but we were always really loose with him and he joked around with us," Steve Kerr said. "I always had a lot of fun with him."

Olson clearly has to remain the "boss" or "disciplinarian" in the basketball family. But he has not forgotten the personal approach for those connected with the basketball program.

"A lot of people don't know the real Lute Olson," said John Streif, Olson's former trainer at Iowa. "He's a guy who loves to go out fishing. He would fish for 12, 13 straight hours if he could. A lot of people wouldn't think Lute would do that. People can't picture that, but it's true."

SALESMAN Look over here, this is a program with a great history, a stable foundation, a bright future. ... It would be a sound deal for you.

No, Olson was not the best car salesman in town, but

he did need a sales pitch inasmuch as 10 of the allotted 18 campus visits already had been used and only one subpar player had been signed during the fall.

"We had only eight campus visits left and we felt we needed to sign six guys," Olson recalled. "What it became, was going out and making the home visits and then trying to get kids interested in a program that was in last place. Once we got kids interested, then we had to say, now we only have a limited amount of visits, can we count on the fact you are interested enough where if you really like it, we will have a chance to be near the top of your list."

1983-84: "WHERE SHALL I BEGIN?"

A bunch of leftovers from the Lindsey year, a player whom nobody else wanted, and a pair of junior college kids were what Olson had to work with.

Lute Olson had plenty of help from his staff throughout the years. Ricky Byrdsong (pictured) is just one of several assistants to eventually take head coaching positions. Others included Kevin O'Neill, Ken Burmeister, Scott Thompson, and Randy Brown.

"I felt comfortable until the first practice when we saw how far we would have to go," Olson said.

On Saturday, October 15, the team hit the floor for the first time with Olson at the controls. A three-hour time slot was scheduled. He usually opts for two or two and a half hours.

The team worked out from 11 a.m. until 2:43, stopping only five minutes for a water break. To prevent excess delay, managers stood around the court with extra balls ready in case they were needed. There would be no time wasted on chasing loose balls.

Instruction 101 covered ball control, ball handling, shooting, rebounding, team offense, team defense, switching, cutting, and offensive motion.

"Where shall I begin?" Olson was thinking.

Normally timed 10 minute drills took 20 for explanations and execution.

"We finally said enough is enough," Olson recalls with a smile — now. "We hadn't gotten through the first third of what we wanted to do in the practice plan. That really hit how difficult a task this would be."

Later, practices went from 2-4:30 p.m. Monday through Saturday with 2-5 p.m. practices on Sunday and hour-long "classroom" instructions about basketball after workouts.

AGUA In order to get a break during practices a player had to make two straight free throws. It sometimes took awhile for a squad which was last in the Pac-10 in 1983 in free-throw percentage.

By the last team scrimmage the Blue team made 17-of-20, while the White team made 15-of-21.

DEBUT At the team's final scrimmage more than 1,000 fans poured into McKale Center. A year earlier, only 100 had bothered to watch.

In an exhibition game against Athletes in Action, Olson started five underclassmen: Michael Tait, Brock Brunkhorst, Pete Williams, Eddie Smith, and Keith Jackson. They didn't fare well, losing 87-72 in front of 6,129 fans.

With two hundred fewer spectators, Olson won the first game of the year, 72-65, over Northern Arizona. Pete Williams tallied 31 points on 12-of-16 shooting from the field, and 7-of-10 from the free throw line. He also added 12 rebounds in his Wildcat debut. The game was tied 32-32 at halftime, but 59 percent shooting in the second half propelled Olson to victory No. 1.

THE SAVING GRACE Although many point to Sean Elliott as the catalyst of Arizona's basketball emergence, Olson

Sean Elliott receives the majority of the credit for jump starting the Arizona program, but Pete Williams (pictured) did more than his share. The JC transfer ignited Olson's first team and then finished his career by leading the Wildcats in rebounds, blocked shots and field goal percentage for two seasons.

is quick to mention Pete Williams' contribution.

The 6-7, 190-pound jumping jack provided Arizona not only outstanding leaping and rebounding skills, but

KERR LIVES WITH SPARKLING IMAGE

Mr. Clean.

Steve Kerr's image in Tucson, and now with the NBA Champion Chicago Bulls, is squeaky. Simply put, he's a fan favorite wherever he goes.

His accuracy from three-point range and his errorless passes would please even the most casual basketball observer, but what has made Kerr so well-liked is his wit, comedic ability, courage and "Opieness."

Just once Kerr announced he wanted to earn a bad boy image before his days in Tucson were complete.

"People think I'm a perfect citizen, but I'm a little bit more colorful than that," Kerr said during his senior campaign. "I drink beer, but I've never been to jail."

Would you like to be arrested?

"I think I would just to shock people," Kerr said in his sarcastic humor. "I would like to see what happens if I picked up a glass and fired it into a wall. What would people do then?"

Probably blame somebody else or look for a supernatural force to excuse the action.

Kerr's no saint. California fans didn't think so after the former sports editor of the Palisades (Calif.) High School paper wrote a guest column in the *Daily Californian* prior to the Wildcats' game against California in Berkeley during the 1988 season.

Just a few of the clips:

■ (To the California band) "Why don't you stay off Pete Newell

Court? You're an embarrassment to Harmon Gym, not to mention Harmon Arena. Or is it Newell Pavilion. Or the Harmon Alameda Coliseum? The Kapp Center? The Granola Dome? or Simply Lou (Campanelli's) Bread Box. Frankly, I think there's one name that would be perfectly suitable — The Harmon Psychiatric Care Unit."

■ (About hated Pac-10 player Reggie Miller of UCLA) "I like you guys because you're the only people in the world who hate Reggie Miller more than myself."

■ (And regarding questions about why he did not attend a "real" school) "I wanted to, but Stanford didn't accept my application."

There is a stab in the heart to any Golden Bear student. The Straw Hat band in Berkeley delivered a pizza with a can of tuna and some hair spray to Kerr in retaliation.

"I figured I would get a reaction," Kerr said at the time. He did, most notably from Campanelli. "You put articles in the campus newspapers of the other schools and it doesn't help any," the humorless Campanelli retorted. "Daily newspapers on campus feed on that stuff, and it adds fuel to the fire. You've got to put yourself above those things, especially a player of his stature."

Lighten up, Lou.

In his spare time Kerr is still trying to convince reporters that Lute wears a toupee. Kerr says he'll be the first one there when Lute decides to overcome his heroin addiction.

a presence that translated into success. The JC transfer from Mount San Antonio College in Walnut, Calif., became the inspiration for not only that first Wildcat

What!?

After being asked several times what his New Year's resolution would be, Kerr decided to spice up the answer a little.

"I would like to help Coach Olson kick his heroin habit," Kerr said, obviously joking.

"The guys said that nobody, other than Steve, could get away with that," Olson said a couple of months ago. "I don't think that was the case. I think Sean (Elliott) would have gotten away with it."

The truth probably is that few others would have made Olson laugh at that. Really.

Few others gained the beloved following Kerr garnered in Tucson. The player many described as "Opie" became a little brother, a best friend, and a son to Wildcat fans.

From the day Kerr's father, Malcolm, the president of American University in Beirut, was assassinated and from the moment of silence granted to the Kerr family before a home game against Arizona State during his freshman year to his departure from Kansas City at the Final Four, few collegians experienced the love affair Kerr felt.

"I just bought a house a couple of blocks from the UA," Kerr said following his NBA championship celebration. "That right there should tell you something about how I still feel about the school."

Kerr concluded his UA basketball career as a second-team all-American, not bad considering hardly anybody else recruited him

seriously out of high school. He was also the NCAA's leading three-point shooter and a second-round pick of the Phoenix Suns.

Steeeeevvvveeee Kerrrrr's clean cut image lives on, even with the World Champion Chicago Bulls.

team, but the program.

"The guy everybody looked to and the guy who was the key to our success was Pete Williams," Olson said. "Pete is still one of the hardest-working guys I have ever dealt with. He had a great team attitude. He had a way of making the game fun and getting the guys together off the court as well as on.

"That is why when people talk about what was the key to the start of the program, was it getting Sean from right here in Tucson? Obviously that was a very critical thing. The point is, we wouldn't have gotten Sean without Pete Williams providing the success he did in his two years. When I talked to Sean prior to the time he signed, he never was going to come here because of the way things had been."

COMING TOGETHER A 51-49 overtime loss to UTEP in the championship game of the Sun Bowl Christmas tournament in El Paso proved progress was being made.

"We really had them beat," Olson said. "We got killed by three late calls that sent it into overtime. UTEP was a very good team, yet we were the better team on the court. The guys really competed hard in a very hostile environment. Instead of their game dropping off, they picked it up. I felt after the Sun Bowl we had turned the corner. I came out thinking, 'It is not there yet, but we are going to be okay.'"

A MOMENT OF SILENCE Forty-eight hours after waking up to the news of his dad's assassination in Beirut, Steve Kerr suited up to play against Arizona State in McKale Center. Although his world had been turned upside down, basketball became a catharsis.

WILDCAT QUIZ

12. When was
Arizona's first
postseason
appearance?

Malcolm Kerr was the president of American University in Beirut, where on January 18, 1984, he was gunned down near his office by Arab militiamen. Steve took residence at the Olson's home for support.

Following a moment of silence prior to the tip-off against the Sun Devils, Kerr, the team's sixth man, came off the bench to hit a 25-foot patented Kerr-jumper.

"Before the game, it was really hard," teammate Brock Brunkhorst said. "You felt like it happened to you. It didn't affect me as much during the game because you are in trying to play, but when he made the shot I had chills. It made you feel better for him. The crowd went crazy. Tucson pretty much adopted him after that."

Kerr's 12 points and the team's 71-49 victory were just footnotes in the record books, but it meant a great deal more in Kerr's healing process.

"The ridiculous thing was that people made a big deal out of the fact I played," Kerr said. "That was the one

Steve Kerr's 25-foot jumper against ASU during his freshman year came after a moment of silence. Kerr's father had died days earlier, the victim of an assassin's bullet in Beirut, Lebanon. Following the ordeal Kerr became a beloved member of the Wildcat family.

thing I could do to get away from my thoughts."

A GIANT The UA was only 11-17 after that first year, but considering how far the program had fallen, Olson believed his instincts had been correct

"I felt this was really a sleeping giant if a staff would come in and really work at the recruiting end of it and really tried to put a solid program together," Olson said. "I felt there were two sleeping giants, Texas in Austin — and here."

Arizona had been awakened.

*Brian Williams, Ed
Stokes, and Sean
Rooks were a force
to be reckoned with.*

1984-1985: THE COMEBACK

The Wildcats were no longer the doormat of the
Pac-10 or a laughingstock around Tucson.

Olson built a foundation with junior college
standouts like Pete Williams and Eddie Smith and then
parlayed their success to recruit the highly visible and
sought-after Craig McMillan, a guard from Cloverdale
(Calif.) High School. Landing McMillan was a coup.
With the talent on the roster drastically improved, the
Wildcats found themselves in the conference
championship race and in the NCAA Tournament.

A MIRACULOUS COMEBACK January 5, 1985: Down 60-53
with 37 seconds left — and without a three-point shot to
bail them out — the Wildcats, to the dismay of the
Arizona State crowd in Tempe, rallied for a 61-60 victory.

A three-point play by Eddie Smith and a jumper from
Morgan Taylor pulled the UA within two. Pete Williams
then deflected a Sun Devil pass to Smith, who raced
down court for a scoop shot. Not only did his shot tie the
game, but he was fouled on the play. Smith made the

Craig McMillan (20) was regarded as the program's first "prize" recruit of the 80s. His steady shot and dependable defense lifted Arizona to NCAA tournament status.

free throw, and ASU's last ditch 25-foot effort fell short to give Arizona a most surprising victory.

"I think that win had a whole lot to do with establishing us as a winning program," Olson said. "That showed we were going to scratch and claw to win. That is important to the continuation of a program."

POST SEASON PLAY The Wildcats appeared in the NCAA tournament for the first time since 1977. Arizona lost 50-41 to Alabama in the first round, but the invitation brought the program back to respectability.

"After seeing the condition of the program and looking at the recruiting necessary, I thought it would be a four- to five-year process," Olson said. "It happened much quicker. Making the NCAA tournament was a great feeling. We knew that would pay off for us. It no

Even though it fell 50-41 to Alabama in the first round of the 1985 NCAA tournament, Arizona began a run of postseason appearances that continues to this day.

longer was the case that we were saying, 'Well, we turned the program around at Iowa. We can turn the program at Arizona as well.' We showed recruits that progress was getting done."

1985-1986: ELLIOTT'S PRESENCE FELT

Arizona welcomed All-American Sean Elliott, shot-blocking and rebounding specialist Anthony Cook, and athletic guard Kenny Lofton. It was time to construct a second story over UA's already solid foundation and first floor.

With these youngsters, the Wildcats took on all challenges the Pac-10 had to offer. Arizona won its first league title — on UCLA's home floor, no less.

In the early going, however, the Wildcats were competitive, but sported a 5-4 record after trips to the Great Alaska Shootout and additional road defeats to Tulsa and Utah.

"When you have inexperience like that you can be competitive, but you are probably going to have a tough time winning the big games, the close games," Olson said. "Inexperience usually shows up at the worst possible time."

It was short-term frustration. Sean Elliott scored a then career-high 28 points, John Edgar grabbed 10 boards and the guard combination of Steve Kerr and Craig McMillan added 33 points against UCLA. The Bruins lost their league championship hopes when Arizona left Pauley Pavilion on the victorious end of an 88-76 outcome.

"Winning that league title was great," Olson said. "There was no way anybody in their right mind could say we would do it with two freshman starters and a sixth man and a guard who had not been offered a scholarship by anybody."

The freshman class of Elliott, Cook, and Lofton won three Pac-10 crowns.

McCLUTCH Practice makes perfect. But even in practice, when the Wildcats simulated a last-second lob to win a game, the play didn't meet with much success.

However, against Oregon State the McClutch shot worked to perfection. Down by one in overtime, McMillan caught up to a deflected lob pass and laid in the shot at the buzzer to give Arizona a 63-62 victory.

"We ran it a lot in practice just in case we needed it in late-game situations," Olson said. "After that happened, Craig said something like we practice it all the time, but it hardly ever works. That is true. It hardly ever does work. You work on a lot of things in practice. Sometimes you wonder if it is worth it, but then something like that happens and it makes it obvious that details are important."

COULD I HAVE YOUR AUTOGRAPH PLEASE Olson has many material souvenirs from that year, but one of his favorite is a UCLA program that his wife, Bobbi, had John Wooden sign the day of Arizona's victory over the Bruins in Pauley Pavilion, marking the school's first league title.

THE RIFLEMAN Chuck Person has gained the reputation as "the Rifleman" with the San Antonio Spurs, but it was his inside presence against Arizona's overmatched front line

WILDCAT QUIZ

13. Who was the first player to score over 1,000 career points?

that sparked Auburn to a 73-63 first round victory in the NCAA tournament. Person's 20 points temporarily put the team's growing accomplishments into the background.

1986-87: WITHOUT KERR

The last gold-medal winning performance by a U.S. collegiate basketball team in international competition came in July 1986 when Olson led a group, including Sean Elliott and Steve Kerr, to the World Championships in Spain.

But Kerr's new jewelry was paid for by a severe knee injury that required reconstructive surgery and forced him to miss the 1986-87 season.

Three starters still remained from the 1986 Pac-10 championship team, but without their point guard, the Wildcats were a lost unit, finishing the year 18-12 after a third-straight first-round defeat.

HOMETOWN HERO

Sean Elliott's No. 32 will forever be a part of Arizona history. His jersey hanging from the rafters in McKale Center.

Taking time out from a busy NBA schedule in 1996, Elliott returned home for a ceremony to retire the first jersey at the UA in any sport.

"That was truly an awesome experience," Elliott said weeks later. "I have been to award things before and I have been given awards before, but that was something special. I thought maybe it would be like when I got the scoring title. I remember on the plane ride back to Seattle that night I was all choked up. My wife was like, 'What is wrong with you?' It was just so overwhelming. It turned out to be a 100 times more than what I thought it would be."

Elliott left his senior season in 1989 as the John Wooden, AP, Kodak, CBS, *Basketball Times*, *Basketball Weekly*, *Hoop Scoop*, and *All-Star Sports Report* National Player of the Year.

He led Arizona in scoring four straight seasons, surpassed Lew Alcindor's Pac-10 scoring mark with 2,555 points, had a career scoring average of 19.2 points and 6.1 rebounds, scored in double figures in 108 consecutive games and 128 of 133 games and helped establish the Wildcat program as one of the elite in the country.

"He's meant a lot in terms of recruiting," Olson said. "There isn't a player in the country that doesn't know who Sean Elliott is. He's opened a lot of doors for us."

Simply put, it's the story of a local kid doing good. He's given back to the community and in return Cholla High School renamed its basketball facility the "Sean Elliott Gymnasium."

A few thoughts on Elliott during his 1989 season:

■ "He's not God, even though I

NCAA TOURNAMENT UTEP, a higher seed, felt miffed at having to travel to Tucson for the first round of the NCAA tournament. Don Haskins' squad proved its point by recording a 98-91 victory in McKale Center.

1987-88: YEAR OF THE WILDCATS

See page 106.

1988-89: LOFTON FALLS DOWN

Many thought Arizona, despite the loss to Oklahoma in the national semifinals, was the best team in the country. The same was said following the 1989 campaign. The Wildcats entered NCAA tournament action as the No. 1 ranked team by both the UPI and AP.

The Wildcats had easily disposed of Pac-10 and other Western foes, while destroying Eastern powers like

think he is sometimes," teammate Jud Buechler said.

■ "I don't know what we call him now," teammate Harvey Mason said. "Last year he was God. This year he's above that."

■ "He's one of the most effective guys I have ever seen," UCLA Coach Jim Harrick said. "He's one of the greatest guys to ever play college basketball. Elliott is virtually unstoppable."

■ "In my opinion he's a first-class NBA player right now," Chicago Bulls' guard Michael Jordan said. "He drives with intensity, can score from inside or outside, and has a determination I haven't seen in a young player in a long time."

Elliott was the No. 3 pick in the 1989 draft, has played with San Antonio and Detroit and has made two NBA all-star appearances.

Sean Elliott's number 32 jersey is the only uniform retired in Arizona's history.

Kenny Lofton's basketball career ended while trying to defend Anderson Hunt's three-pointer in the 1989 Sweet 16. He has since become one of the best players in Major League Baseball, as evidenced by his appearance in the 1996 All-Star game.

Pittsburgh, Temple, and Villanova. Elliott was the guiding force. He scored 32 points and grabbed 15 rebounds against UNLV, logged a career-high 36 points against Pittsburgh, and 31 vs Villanova.

By the time the season was complete Arizona posted a 29-4 record. Its worst loss had been 79-72 to North Carolina in Charlotte. The UA advanced to the Sweet 16.

REVENGE NOT POSSIBLE There is little substitute for losing in the Final Four, but Arizona traveled to Norman for an ounce of redemption against No. 5 Oklahoma. Despite more steals, fewer turnovers, a better shooting percentage, and a closer rebounding margin, the same result occurred — an 82-80 loss.

Matt Muehlebach emerged as the team's next great floor leader with 18 points and one turnover in 36 minutes.

ROMPING THE BRUINS Lost in Sean Elliott's Pac-10 scoring record was the job Arizona did on UCLA, the only team close to challenging the UA in the Pac-10.

By the time Elliott's record was in the books, Arizona had built a 62-33 lead with 14 minutes left. A 21-4 spree

PLAY NO. 6—A RECORD BREAKER

February 18, 1989—Arizona Coach Lute Olson thought, just for a second, about what would be the best play.

Play No. 6.

Play No. 6 called for Sean Elliott, the 1989 College Player of the Year, to be isolated on one side of the court, while his teammates practically huddled on the other.

In essence, Olson told Elliott to go one-on-one with anyone who dared guard him. UCLA had nobody up to the challenge. Arizona won, 102-64.

That was not the story.

On this day Elliott broke a 20-year old conference record previously held by UCLA's Lew Alcindor (Kareem Abdul-Jabbar). The Tucson product needed 34 points entering the game.

Under Olson's system, at that time, few had the green light. Elliott was told on this occasion to "Go, Go, Go."

With 20 points by halftime, all eyes were on the record.

"I saw him looking up throughout the game (at the scoreboard)," teammate Anthony Cook said. "He was watching the points after awhile."

Two three-pointers in the opening minutes made the record a virtual lock. The crowd sensed the moment, counting down the points.

"At that point we tried to get him isolated and let him just go," Olson said.

Play No. 6.

With 31 points, Elliott missed back-to-back three-pointers; the crowd growned.

An acrobatic field goal moments later tied the Pac-10 scoring record. The crowd started chanting "We're No. 1," signifying the one point needed. Elliott even took some time to think about how the record would be broken.

"I was going to drive the lane for a dunk, but they were helping out pretty good," Elliott said. "I knew I couldn't do that."

The drive he wanted ended with a foul, sending Elliott to the free throw line — needing one.

"I concentrated as hard as I could," Elliott said. "I just said to myself that you are going to knock them down."

Ironically, when the ball went through the net it was a Bruin, Pooh Richardson, who first congratulated Elliott.

"I said, 'Congratulations. Keep going. Do what you have to,'" Richardson said. "I thought it was a great thing for someone to achieve."

Afterwards a trophy was presented honoring the feat. Elliott's name was boldly placed on it, but something was missing.

"We haven't put the point total on because there's a lot more to come," Olson said.

Elliott finished his Arizona career with 2,555 points.

to open the second half finished off UCLA. The 102-64 loss is the worst in Bruin history. Elliott wound up with 35 points, seven rebounds and 11 assists. Cook had 19 points, and Jud Buechler added 13 rebounds.

ELLIOTT-FERRY Again lost in a battle for the nation's No. 1 ranking was the personal battle between Elliott and Duke's Danny Ferry, the two players regarded as the best in the country.

Ferry finished with 29 points and 12 rebounds in the clash at the Meadowlands in New Jersey, but Elliott's three-pointer in the final minute propelled Arizona to a 77-75 victory and a claim to the top-spot.

ANOTHER RUN AT THE FINAL FOUR There is not much to do in Boise, Idaho, so the Wildcats had their fun on the court, scoring 23 field goals in the paint en route to a 94-60 pasting of Robert Morris. Elliott and Cook combined for 52 points in the first-round NCAA encounter.

Clemson wasn't much more challenging, especially in the second half, as Muehlebach and Elliott led the way in a 94-68 win. Muehlebach had 19 points and zero turnovers, while Elliott had another ho-hum 25 points.

DOWN FOR THE COUNT Most remember Kenny Lofton's last-second flop to the floor while Anderson Hunt nailed a three-pointer to give UNLV an emotional 68-67 victory over Arizona with four seconds left.

Elliott's 22 points and 14 rebounds were lost as he played the final game of his Wildcat career.

WILDCAT QUIZ

14. What positions did Mo and Stewart Udall play?

LOFTON-BASEBALL STAR Lofton is tearing up the base paths in the American League, but he was also good at thievery while at the UA.

Until the 1995 season, Lofton held Arizona's record for steals with 200. He also emerged as an efficient point guard while Kerr was out with an injury and following his graduation.

Yet Lofton seemed to have little future in athletics. Sure, Elliott, and probably Cook would excel in the NBA, but Lofton needed help — and a change of venue.

Upon finishing his basketball career Lofton turned to baseball full-time at the UA and then later played in the minor-league systems.

"Kenny probably still feels he would have made it in the NBA. If he would have made it, I think it would have been a marginal thing," Olson said. "The best thing to happen to Kenny was baseball."

Lofton is now considered one of the top 10 players in the game — and is contracted to make nearly $4 million per year.

1990-93: EXPECTATION OVERKILL

The Wildcats have looked down on Pac-10 competition with seven league titles in the past 11 years.

There was so much expected from the Wildcats following the 1988 and 1989 seasons. Getting to the Final Four, being ranked No. 1, and easily winning conference championships just whet the appetites of many.

Winning the Pac-10 and making it into the NCAA tournament brought boos and criticism instead of pats on the back and praise. "You guys are better than this, come on" seemed to be the general tone.

By the end of this four-year run, the Wildcats lost back-to-back first round games. The last came against a bunch of "surfers" from Santa Clara. National ads mocked Arizona; local jokes were plentiful.

"One of the burdens those guys had to deal with was the tremendous popularity of the teams from 1986-89," Olson said. "The expectations of everybody was so high. … I like to use the example of a car salesman selling 16 cars one month. Your quota doesn't drop to 14 cars the next month. If you sold 16 last month, then you should be able to sell 17 this month and 18 after that."

With players like Chris Mills, a Pac-10 MVP; Sean Rooks, the school's seventh-leading scorer; Jud Buechler, now a member of the Chicago Bulls; Khalid Reeves; Brian Williams; and Ed Stokes the Wildcats were expected — demanded — to be national-championship caliber.

The media said so, the fans and even the former Wildcats who played pickup games with these guys thought greatness was in store.

■ "It's incredible. These guys are so good," Kerr said.

"They can put a number of NBA prospects on the floor at the same time. There is Rooks, Mills, Stokes. They are potential lottery picks. And Khalid (Reeves), judging from what I've seen, he can really play."

■ "I think they will be pretty damn good," Elliott said. "There won't be too many teams that can play with the big guys that they have here."

■ "We know we have the potential," Chris Mills said. "We just have to stick together."

Potential. Lottery picks.

Those words are a kiss of death when you lose to East Tennessee State and Santa Clara.

"There was a lot of pressure just because of the success and because of the way they were accepted after the group with Sean Elliott and Steve Kerr," Olson said. "I think it put a lot of pressure on them to win, put a lot of pressure on them to hold on to that popularity Arizona basketball had. If you go to the Final Four in 1988 and in 1989 you lose with a fluke when Kenny got knocked down, then all of a sudden you are a failure if you don't get to the Final Four. That is asinine."

1989-90: GRAVE ROBBERS

SUMMER VACATION Before starting the 1989-90 season the group packed its bags for a 22-day trip to Europe, which featured stops in France, West Germany, Spain, and the Canary Islands.

Between Wayne Womack shattering a backboard, a near bench-clearing brawl against a West German team,

Following the 1989 season the staff and players left for a 22-day tour of Europe, logging a 6-3 record and plenty of sun and fun as Sean Rooks and Wayne Womack could attest.

and a try at bull fighting, the Wildcats completed the tour with a 6-3 record and a glimpse of the future.

Completed questionnaire results from the trip:

Best Game — Beating the West German Nationals

Favorite City/town — Paris

Best Dinner — Hotel Principe Vergara, Madrid: Romaine salad, beef, bread

Best looking women — Spain

Best shopper — Bobbi Olson

Friendliest people — West Germany

Most memorable sight — (tie), Eiffel tower, Rhone castles, girl in purple bikini on Gran Canaria

Best cliff jumper — Craig McMillan

Most mellow traveler — Assistant coach Jessie Evans

Worst Traveler — (Censored)

ON THE ROAD   In an eight-day stretch (February 18-25) the Wildcats played at UNLV (losing 95-87), returned home, traveled to California (winning 93-68 thanks to 75 percent shooting in the first half), then Stanford (winning 80-61), returned home, and then traveled to Duke (losing 78-76).

GRAVE DIGGERS   Arizona came "back from the grave," as Olson put it, following two straight losses to open the 1989 Pac-10 season in Oregon to claim a share of the Pac-10 title.

RED FACED   After a 79-67 victory over South Florida in the first round the Wildcats fell to Alabama 77-55. Arizona's

Togetherness — the reason for success, especially early on, was closeness. Brian David, Wayne Womack, Sean Rooks, Jud Buechler, Ron Curry, and Bruce Fraser remain in touch to this day.

Chris Mills (42) was a big-time catch following his transfer from Kentucky. The UA forward was named the Pac-10's Player of the Year his senior season.

big front line was outrebounded 40-27. The Wildcats were 25-7 on the season.

1990-91: MILLING AROUND

The Wildcats had Kentucky transfer Chris Mills in uniform for the start of the season after filing a petition with the NCAA for immediate playing a year earlier. The NCAA said "no."

The Wildcats were not short-handed any longer with the "Tucson Skyline" of Sean Rooks, Brian Williams, and Ed Stokes, combined with guard leadership from Matt Muehlebach and Matt Othick.

NIT CHAMPS Mills and Rooks cut off all the lanes in the preseason NIT tournament to give Arizona a convincing championship, culminating with an 89-77 victory over Arkansas in Madison Square Garden.

Mills earned NIT MVP honors with his 29-point, 13-rebound outing against the Razorbacks. Rooks had 31 points, while Othick had 15 assists, five steals, and only two turnovers in the two New York City games.

NO. 1 For the first time in two years the Wildcats arrived back from the NIT tournament as the top-ranked team in the country. That honor lasted until Shaquille O'Neal

A year before, Shaquille O'Neal had dominated the Wildcats in LSU's 92-82 win over No. 1 ranked Arizona, but the tables were turned during the 1992 season as Ed Stokes & Co. quieted "Shaq."

In the last eight years Arizona has averaged 26 wins per season, posted a 133-29 record in league play and a 243-53 overall mark, the nation's best during this period. In 13 years in McKale Center the Wildcats are 175-23 (.883).

scored 29 points, grabbed 14 rebounds, and blocked six shots in LSU's 92-82 home victory.

NCAA ACTION Seeded No. 2 in the West, the Wildcats defeated St. Francis 93-80 in the first round as Matt Othick made 8 of 10 shots for a career-high 25 points.

Next came BYU, playing close to home in Salt Lake City. The Cougars had 7-foot, six-inch freshman center Shawn Bradley, but Arizona countered with three giants

Khalid Reeves' broken thumb prevented his full participation against Seton Hall in 1991. Arizona lost 81-77 following NCAA tournament victories over St. Francis and BYU.

inside to pull off a 76-61 victory. Williams led the Wildcats with 24 points, 11 rebounds and three blocks. Bradley fouled out with 10 points.

Reeves' broken thumb spelled doom for the Wildcats in the Sweet 16. There were 15 lead changes when Arizona and Seton Hall met. It was nearly 16 when Othick's three-pointer with seconds remaining fell short. Seton Hall prevailed, 81-77. The Wildcats concluded the season 28-7.

1991-92: WINNING STREAK OVER

Tough Times.

Arizona's 71-game home court winning streak came to an end as Darrick Martin's buzzer-beating shot gave UCLA an 89-87 victory on January 11.

Add to that a two-game losing streak entering the first round of the NCAA tournament and Arizona appeared to be on a downward cycle. The Wildcats

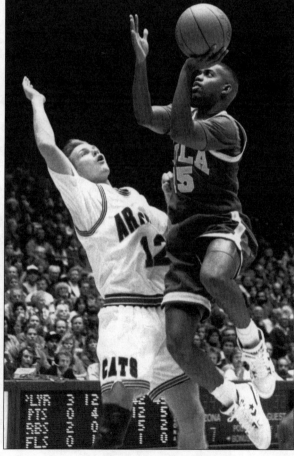

Darrick Martin's last-second shot ended Arizona's 71-game home court winning streak. The UA lost 89-87 to UCLA. The streak had begun December 4, 1987.

Team captains Matt Othick, Sean Rooks, and Wayne Womack still look back at how the 1991-92 season and their college careers came to a close — with three straight defeats, including a loss to East Tennessee State in the first round of the NCAA tournament.

were 13-5 in league play, finishing behind top 10 teams UCLA and USC.

The third loss came against a team wrongly seeded 14th. East Tennessee State was too fleet of foot for Arizona's big men and Othick had his worst game ever, being shutout from the scoring column after taking six shots. The Buccaneers' 87-80 victory began a slew of criticism about the UA's first round difficulties.

71-GAME HOME WINNING STREAK

1987-88 Season		Opponent	Score	Opponent	Score
Opponent	Score	25 Pittsburgh	88-62	49 E. Tennessee St.	84-37
1 Long Beach State	94-62	26 Oregon State	85-64	50 Western Illinois	90-51
2 Pepperdine	73-68	27 Oregon	95-71	51 Long Beach State	95-68
3 NAU	77-59	28 Villanova	75-67	52 Providence	99-87
4 Ark.-Little Rock	77-53	29 Stanford	72-52	53 Pepperdine	80-66
5 Michigan State	78-58	30 California	86-59	54 Iowa State	102-77
6 Duke	91-85	31 USC	93-70	55 USC	87-85
7 California	80-51	32 UCLA	102-64	56 UCLA	82-77
8 Stanford	90-65	33 Arizona State	109-74	57 Washington State	84-71
9 USC	92-48	*1989-90 Season*		58 Washington	85-56
10 UCLA	86-74	34 NAU	84-37	59 Arizona State	71-50
11 Arizona State	99-59	35 Miami (Fla.)	83-53	60 California	100-63
12 Illinois	78-70	36 Penn State	74-55	61 Duke	103-92
13 Oregon	89-57	37 Purdue	85-66	62 Stanford	89-51
14 Oregon State	77-62	38 California	71-70	63 Oregon State	82-67
15 Washington State	79-41	39 Washington	65-51	64 Oregon	107-65
16 Washington	89-71	40 Washington State	81-61	*1991-92 Season*	
17 California	88-64	41 Oklahoma	78-74	65 LSU	87-67
18 Stanford	97-83	42 Stanford	68-61	66 NAU	122-81
19 Oregon State	93-67	43 USC	95-70	67 Evansville	83-76
1988-89 Season		44 UCLA	83-74	68 Rutgers	103-80
20 New Mexico	80-67	45 Arizona State	71-50	69 New Orleans	82-64
21 UNLV	86-75	46 Oregon	84-58	70 Santa Clara	79-60
22 Washington State	76-59	47 Oregon State	87-60	71 USC	107-68
23 Washington	116-61	*1990-91 Season*			
24 Loyola-Chicago	106-82	48 Austin Peay	122-80		

1992-93: SURFER DUDES HANG 10 AT EXPENSE OF UA

Ask anybody about this year and two words will come to mind — Santa Clara.

The "surfer dudes" outplayed an Arizona team that had Chris Mills in foul trouble for much of the game. Final: 64-61 in Salt Lake City. It represented only the second time in NCAA history that a No. 2 seed had fallen in the first round.

Talk of jinx, black cats, and voodoo seemed to be some of the explanations for Arizona's 30.9 percent field goal shooting. The Wildcat players, themselves, simply said, "We choked."

Despite winning Pac-10 titles, Chris Mills and members of teams from the 1990-93 seasons have been tagged more for first-round NCAA defeats.

Just like that a 24-4 record, a season that had featured a 19-game winning streak, Chris Mills' becoming the Pac-10's Player of the Year, and another league title was cast aside this time because of — Santa Clara.

1993-94: ANOTHER FINAL FOUR

See page 119.

1994-95: FRUSTRATION HITS HIGH

Maintaining any kind of rhythm was virtually impossible for one reason or another throughout the season.

Whether it was the NCAA ineligibility of Ben Davis and Damon Stoudamire, or from injures to Miles Simon (finger), Joseph Blair (ankle and suspension), and Corey Williams (eye), bad luck, poor timing, and maybe even bad karma, the Wildcats were just not ready for a repeat Final Four performance.

The Wildcats' season started with a 72-70 loss to Minnesota in the Great Alaska Shootout and ended abruptly with a first-round loss to Miami of Ohio in the

Ray Owes emerged as one of the Pac-10's top inside threats in 1995, averaging 15.1 points and 8.1 rebounds per game.

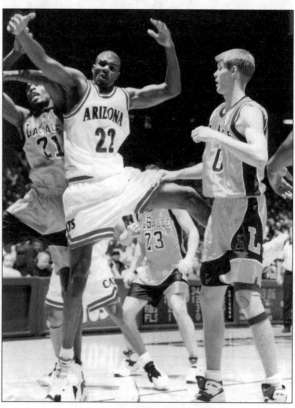

NCAA tournament.

Sure, Arizona posted its 11th straight trip to the NCAA tournament and finished with a 23-8 record, but another first-round defeat, combined with the circumstances of such an ordeal overshadowed another successful regular season run.

PLAY ON MONDAY The Wildcats broke out shirts with the season's motto clearly visible. A December academic suspension to Blair, followed by a Pac-10 season opening loss to ASU and a 71-61 loss to UCLA in McKale Center, the second such double-digit defeat in the Olson era at home, became too much to overcome.

There were plenty of highlights, including a miraculous comeback at Washington State, where Arizona was down by 10 with 1:18 remaining in regulation.

Thanks largely to Miles Simon's picking off a Cougar pass and turning it into a tying lay-up, the Wildcats claimed an unthinkable 114-111 victory.

STOUDAMIRE'S SWAN SONG A year later Damon Stoudamire would be the NBA's Rookie of the Year after being selected seventh overall by expansion Toronto. During his senior season with Arizona, Stoudamire was a consensus all-American. He averaged 22.8 points, 4.3 rebounds, and 7.3 assists per game.

Stoudamire reached the 40-point barrier twice, recording 45 in an 89-83 overtime victory over Stanford and 40 in the win against Washington State.

The heralded point guard's collegiate career could hardly have had a more disappointing end. Not only was he declared ineligible for the final regular-season home game (an Arizona loss), but he was unsure of his status for the first-round game in the NCAA tournament for much of the week — all the result of a plane ticket allegedly purchased by his father from a sports agent.

The mental strain was obvious as Stoudamire and the Wildcats struggled. In the loss to Miami, of Ohio, Davis was declared ineligible by the NCAA. Add Blair's badly sprained ankle and that marked doom for Arizona in the 71-62 loss.

Stoudamire clearly recovered from that disappointment with his landslide NBA Rookie of the Year award.

"The reason Damon has made it where he has is because of his tremendous work ethic," Olson said. "In the summer guys were playing pickup games or getting into leagues. Damon always had his schedule for the summer, lining out 'these are the things I have to work on.'

"His summers became more individual work. He would think nothing of going out while in Portland and spending four hours a day extending his range on his

WILDCAT QUIZ

15. Who owns Arizona's school record for rebounds in a game with 26 and led the nation as a senior for fouls?

Following NCAA scrutiny Damon Stoudamire was permitted to play in Arizona's first round game against Miami of Ohio, but mental fatigue, the ineligibility of Ben Davis, and Joseph Blair's injured ankle could not prevent a major upset.

three-point shot or ball handling. You are not going to find somebody who is more determined to be successful than Damon. You will never find anybody with a bigger heart than Damon. You hear a lot of people who say he has the heart of a lion. I think that is it in stone."

1995-96: GIVE CATS CREDIT

Sooner or later people will learn that the more the Arizona basketball program is underappreciated the chances of success increase two-fold.

So was the case again.

Arizona was given instant motivation when it was excluded from the preseason top 25 poll. The slight snapped the longest current streak in the country — 141 weeks.

Saying UCLA had reclaimed the rights to the West by winning the national championship the previous season was like telling Arizona what it had accomplished over the past decade meant little.

When the preseason NIT committee failed to give Arizona a second-round home game, sending it instead to Fayetteville, Ark. just prompted more motivation.

When Arizona lost back-to-back games in the Bay area to open league play, it was a diagnosis of doom.

Olson's group rose from the proverbial coffin repeatedly during the 1995-96 season to shock virtually everyone. Before the season was complete Arizona was back in the NCAA tournament, advanced past the first round, into the Sweet 16, and was a play or two from reaching the Final Four in the Meadowlands.

Not bad for a team underrated all season and a squad that lost Joseph Blair, its leading scorer and rebounder early in the season, due to an academic ineligibility. Arizona finished with a 26-7 record.

THE BIG APPLE The New York media was enthralled with the play of Georgetown point guard Allan Iverson, and rightly so, but the "team" play of Arizona led to an NIT preseason championship. The Wildcats whipped the Hoyas 91-81 in Madison Square Garden.

Michael Dickerson showed he could put up some big numbers in 1996, but more consistency is being asked of him in the years to come.

Not much was expected of the 1996 Wildcats, but after four triumphs in the preseason NIT Arizona brought back the trophy and newfound respect.

Iverson's 40 points in the title game were impressive, but even more so were the 17-point efforts of Joseph Blair, Ben Davis, and Miles Simon and the assist-making and defense of Reggie Geary.

In the four-game sweep, Arizona defeated Long Beach State 91-57 behind a 19-point outing from Michael Dickerson and an 18-point, nine-rebound performance from Davis. That followed with a road trip to Bud Walton Arena in Arkansas where the young Razorbacks were taught a stern lesson during an 83-73 Wildcat win. Geary's 12 assists aided Arizona's travel plans to New York City.

Once in the middle of the skyscrapers, the Wildcats dismantled the big bodies of Michigan 86-79. Miles Simon scored 21 points and Davis registered 17 points and 12 rebounds.

CROWD PLEASER When 14,638 fans entered McKale Center to watch the Wildcats defeat UCLA, it marked

McKALE CENTER ATTENDANCE FIGURES

Year	Record	Total	Per Game	Year	Record	Total	Per Game
1972-73	4-1	64,975	12,995	1984-85	12-3	163,980	10,932
1973-74	14-1	184,275	12,285	1985-86	16-0	179,008	11,188
1974-75	13-1	159,096	.11,364	1986-87	10-5	190,800	12,720
1975-76	16-0	179,523	11,220	1987-88	19-0	252,649	13,297
1976-77	16-0	199,130	12,446	1988-89	14-0	190,675	13,620
1977-78	12-3	172,428	11,495	1989-90	14-0	190,949	13,639
1978-79	13-2	174,831	11,655	1990-91	17-0	235,051	13,826
1979-80	10-6	181,428	11,339	1991-92	15-1	222,347	13,884
1980-81	10-7	160,651	9,450	1992-93	14-1	208,185	13,879
1981-82	6-8	115,272	8,234	1993-94	14-1	209,592	13,973
1982-83	4-10	87,136	6,224	1994-95	11-3	199,589	14,257
1983-84	7-7	102,163	7,297	1995-96	13-3	228,064	14,254

the largest home crowd in the Olson era. That is saying something, considering the Wildcats have led the Pac-10 in home attendance for 12 years.

But, after all, when Olson arrived he promised a Wildcat basketball ticket would be valuable.

"In Coach Olson's second year we only had two or three sellouts. That was a big deal for us," Bruce Fraser said. "Back then we couldn't give our tickets away. Steve (Kerr) and I looked at one another when Coach Olson would speak at banquets and tell people they better get tickets because pretty soon they won't be able to be bought. We laughed about that.

"That was his standard speech. Before long he made us believe. It's amazing he did it in such a short amount of time. Steve and I thought about making the investment and buying four seats. We should have, but we didn't have the funds back then as students."

Since the 1987-88 season, the Wildcats are 131-9 (93.6 percent) at home, 55-2 in non-conference games.

500 PLUS Olson earned his 500th career victory when Miles Simon made a three-quarter court shot at the buzzer to defeat Cincinnati at the 7-Up Shootout Classic in Veterans Memorial Coliseum in Phoenix on February 11.
Win No. 1: Dec. 1, 1973, 84-55 over Puget Sound
Win No. 100: Feb. 3, 1979, 97-71 over Minnesota
Win No. 200: Feb. 25, 1984, 69-58 over Oregon State
Win No. 300: March 27, 1988, 70-52 over North Carolina
Win No. 400: Feb. 13, 1992, 94-72 over Washington State
Win No. 500: Feb. 11, 1996, 79-76 over Cincinnati

FORGETTING THE PAST Of course NCAA tournament time means media questions about first-round failures and defensive answers from members of the basketball

Arizona Coach Lute Olson picked up his 300th Arizona win in the championship game of the Fiesta Bowl Classic, a 79-70 victory over Rutgers. On Miles Simon's 65-foot shot at the buzzer at the 7 Up Shootout in Phoenix, Olson notched his 500th career win in Arizona's shocking 79-76 upset over Cincinnati.

program.

With the Miami of Ohio debacle the year earlier, too many critics had conveniently forgotten about Arizona's two Final Four appearances during an eight-year span. This time, though, the Wildcats made believers out of the naysayers. The UA routed Valparaiso, 90-51. The Wildcats shot 65.6 percent from the field en route to a 51-15 lead at halftime.

Two days later Arizona was scheduled to take on Iowa, but first the team had to reach Tempe's Activity Center. Several players got stuck in a parking elevator prior to the game. That was not a sign of things to come as Arizona defeated the Hawkeyes, 87-73.

Geary had 13 assists and scored 16 points, while Davis collected 14 rebounds and 17 points for his 17th double-double of the season.

SWEET 16 Facing Kansas in Denver's McNichols Arena proved to be no easy task. The Jayhawks came in with two powerful front line players, a sharpshooter on the perimeter, and Jacque Vaughn, whom many touted as the best point guard in the country.

The large Kansas contingent also did not help — the Jayhawks that is. Arizona built a 12-point first half lead before Kansas responded to take a 72-60 lead with 6:15 left in the game against an apparently fatigued Wildcat squad.

Arizona recovered, thanks largely to nine points from Michael Dickerson, but a pair of Vaughn free throws with 9.1 seconds remaining propelled Kansas into the regional finals.

Reggie Geary made a name for himself by playing defense and skying for highlight-reel dunks.

Final Four Seasons

1988: YEAR OF THE WILDCATS

Charismatic center Tom Tolbert drew people to him with his charm and his capacity to say the bizarre.

What he came up with on October 15, 1987, was a little out of touch — even for him. At least, that is what college basketball fans outside of the city limits had to be thinking.

"Tucson's going to see something they haven't seen in a long time," Tolbert said. "Everybody realizes that this could be a year for the national championship."

Say what? Let's clean out the ears first before you repeat that, Tom.

Anthony Cook led the Wildcats in blocked shots four straight years. He is also the school's leader in a game (seven), a season (84) and career (278).

The Associated Press has ranked Arizona No. 17 to begin the season, and Tolbert is declaring the possibility of a national championship run to Kansas City.

See you in the funny farm.

Even the ultra conservative Jud Buechler chimed in with a boast.

"We should lose no more than two games (in the Pac-10), and they should be flukes," Buechler proclaimed.

Well, as it turned out Arizona players backed up the chatter with trouncing victories. The Wildcats recorded a 35-3 record on their way to the school's first Final Four appearance.

In the process Arizona defeated teams by a margin of 22.2 points. The three losses came at New Mexico, at Stanford, and against Oklahoma in the National semifinals.

STRUCK FAME IN ALASKA With an "us against the world" mentality the Arizona basketball team put away its swimming trunks and short sleeved shirts and packed big burly jackets for Anchorage and the field in the Great Alaska Shootout.

As it turned out, the Wildcats were the only ones feeling at home. Michigan, a team regarded by Dick Vitale as the national-champion-to-be, and Syracuse, the Associated Press' top-ranked team, fell victim to Arizona's unselfish and devastating style.

With a 133-78 victory over Duquesne as a prelude of things to come, Arizona found the national prestige it had lacked for a decade with three convincing wins.

A band of all-American hot dogs from Michigan looked down on the Wildcats. This Bill Frieder team was not going to give in to Arizona's idealism — or so it thought.

With Gary Grant, the nation's premier point guard, controlling the action, Michigan fell behind 39-30 at halftime.

Before the Wolverines could see where the next pass was going, Arizona had won 79-64, setting up a showdown with the Orangemen. Syracuse entered with a front line of Derrick Coleman, Steve Thompson, and Rony Seikaly.

Arizona countered with Sean Elliott, Anthony Cook, and Tom Tolbert. But it was Joe Turner who wound up being better than all, scoring 10 points and grabbing seven rebounds off the bench to help provide an 80-68 Great Alaska Shoot-out Championship.

CONQUERING HEROES Upon the team's arrival at Tucson International Airport, nearly 400 fans were waiting outside the gate chanting "U of A, U of A."

It would not be a one-time deal. Airport security had its hands full with every Wildcat return trip. Passengers

Seldom-used Joe Turner turned out to be the star of the Great Alaska Shootout Championship game with 10 points and seven rebounds in Arizona's 80-68 victory over Syracuse.

with standby arrangements just shook their heads, wondering what all the excitement was about.

They would soon know.

HOME WINNING STREAK A 94-62 victory over Long Beach State on December 4 began a string of 71 straight victories in McKale Center that lasted until the 1992 season.

GREEN CREATURE BECOMES HOUSEHOLD NAME

Gumbymania hit Tucson like a virus in 1988.

The bench of eventual superstars displayed symptoms of enthusiasm, excitement and support. There was no cure — and no limit to how far Gumbyitis would go.

Reserves Matt Muehlebach, Sean Rooks, Jud Buechler, Harvey Mason, Mark Georgeson, Craig Bergman, and Brian David always had something going on. The captain of this unit was graduate assistant coach Bruce Fraser, who was one year removed from his Wildcat playing career.

It was Fraser who started the fad, which prompted T-shirts, large green inflatable Gumby dolls and talk all across the land. Before long the children's hit show featuring Gumby, the often abused, green, stretchy figure, and his pal Pokey, became a household name.

The phenomenon had started a year earlier when Fraser, feeling a bit underappreciated and underused, stuffed a small Gumby figure into a sock during games. Only Gumby's head and arms would stick out.

"Any athlete has a difficult time when he is used to playing a lot and then forced to sit and watch," said Fraser, who spends the summers working with Sean Elliott's basketball camps. "It's tough to warm up for an hour, sit for two hours and then come in and play in the final couple of minutes. It is basically scrub time. To put a light on that I told Steve (Kerr) that I felt like the biggest Gumby in the world. So I started putting this little Gumby in my sock."

The first appearance of Gumby came at a most inopportune occasion when "I drove to the basket in a game and was fouled. I hit the court," Fraser said. "The Gumby fell out. The referee picked it up thinking a fan threw it on the court. I had to retrieve it after the game. That is how the whole Gumby thing got started."

The following year Fraser worked as a graduate assistant with the scout team, a squad outclassed and overshadowed by the likes of Kerr and Sean Elliott. Fraser declared his unit "Gumbies."

"Since I was a coach I couldn't tell them to wear a Gumby in their socks, plus I don't think Coach Olson would have gone for that," Fraser said.

What the Gumbies eventually became was the best cheerleading squad in the country, even ousting the Dallas Cowboy girls for that honor.

The bench warmers had it down to a choreographed art form. They would box each other out during timeouts so their jersey names could make television broadcasts;

TV STARS Every game was televised, many nationally. By this time even Bill Cosby (with the highly successful Cosby Show) had to take a back seat to Wildcat basketball.

"National television was so critical to us," Olson said. "Outside of the West, nobody had any clue what was happening down here. Once you get on ESPN and have national writers there and national writers watching the tournament, that was an important step for us."

orchestrated three-point signals were raised before the ball would even sink through the nets, and, in unison, the bench would bow to the moves Elliott made on the court.

In their spare time the Gumbies tried to sneak M&M's or other snacks onto the bench or put soda in the water bottles. Nothing was sacred. Georgeson, on a dare, even showed up to games wearing just a jock strap underneath his sweats because he knew playing time was unlikely.

But the Gumbies were more than just a sideshow. They worked on scout teams to prepare the starters and lightened the mood when practices became tedious.

As scout team members they were responsible for learning opposing teams' offenses and defenses in 10 minutes or less. In preparation for a game against Illinois, Illini plays quickly underwent a name change.

Instead of a play called a "double," the Gumbies transformed it into "Double Cheeseburger." A play to the center was a "Whopper." A play that went to the team's top shooter was referred to as a "Big Mac" and to the small guard "The Kid's Meal."

By the time many of these Gumbies stopped being abused they turned into successful college and pro players. Rooks and

Buechler are still in the NBA.

There have been no sightings of Gumbies since.

Sean Rooks was one of the more vocal Gumbies.

From a ratings perspective, Arizona television broadcasts bested network programming in Tucson.

EMOTIONAL HOMECOMING Upon his appearance in Carver-Hawkeye Arena the Iowa faithful stood up and cheered for their former coach with chants of "Lute! Lute! Lute!"

Those same fans were not as gracious after the Wildcats left the court with a 66-59 victory.

"They knew I really wanted this one," Olson said. "You don't spend nine years of your life in a place where you know all those people and have all of those great memories without coming back feeling a bit special."

Steve Kerr completed the 1987-88 regular season with 29 turnovers in 30 games. He had 11 games without a turnover.

NO. 1 Following a Kentucky loss to Alabama and Arizona's 110-71 victory at Washington to open Pac-10 play, the UA became the top-ranked team in the country. The Wildcats had shot 70 percent from the field and had eight players reach double figures in the win over the Huskies.

The No. 1 ranking was waiting by the time the team bussed to Pullman two days later.

"I thought we were going to have a good team coming back this year," Kerr said. "I never thought we would be No. 1."

The Wildcats made certain they remained the King of the Country against Washington State. Despite a vocal and enthusiastic crowd ready to knock off the No. 1 team, Arizona raced to a 21-5 lead before settling for an 89-55 win.

FIESTA TIME The Fiesta Bowl Classic in McKale Center was more like a mini Final Four: No. 1 Arizona, No. 8 Florida, No. 9 Duke, and tradition-rich Michigan State.

It was a hot ticket. Media from *Sports Illustrated*, *People*, *The Washington Post*, the *New York Times* and

'88 WILDCATS PLAYED TO RAVE REVIEWS

The following are some excerpts of what was being said about the 1988 run to the Final Four:

■ "I look at the Pac-10 right now where Arizona is just in another class. It's like comparing a Rolls Royce to a bunch of Chevrolets," ESPN broadcaster Dick Vitale proclaimed.

■ "In the history of college basketball, Arizona had the finest month of December of any team," CBS analyst Billy Packer said after Wildcat victories over highly ranked Michigan, Syracuse, Iowa, and Duke.

■ "They ran us down and beat us consistently," Duquesne Coach Jim Satalin said following a 133-78 loss. "They play with an inordinate amount of confidence."

■ "They're just too good for us," Michigan Coach Bill Frieder said.

■ "We played man-to-man (defense) because they're death on zones," Syracuse Coach Jim Boeheim said.

■ "At the outset of the year it was

obvious that Arizona would be good," Iowa Coach Dr. Tom Davis said. "They had so many dimensions: the backcourt, the frontcourt, the bench."

■ "Arizona isn't one of those teams which settles into a groove five minutes into the game," Washington State Coach Kelvin Sampson said. "At 19:59, they're ready to play."

■ "Every time we tried to help out or over-commit they took advantage of it with good passing," Oregon State Coach Ralph Miller said. "We took it on the chin."

■ "They are going to whip more people like they did us," USC Coach George Raveling said. "The paramedics will be back for some more bodies."

■ "It was a nightmare," Arizona State Coach Steve Patterson said. "It was like we were going in slow motion and they were in fast forward. It is something special to see Arizona do what they do. You have to hail to the victors."

many more were on hand to document the event.

After Arizona disposed of Michigan State, 78-58, and Duke got past Florida, 93-70, a classic matchup was set.

Arizona vs Duke.

Sean Elliott vs Danny Ferry.

The Wildcats won both featured matchups. Elliott scored 31 points and grabbed nine rebounds in a 91-85 victory.

THE PIT The noise? Blaring. The crowd? Ready. The Lobos? Victorious. The celebration? Newsworthy.

Craig McMillan's desperation shot at the buzzer fell off the rim, prompting New Mexico fans to mob the floor after a 61-59 victory in The Pit.

Despite shooting 39 percent from the field, the Wildcats rallied from a 16-point deficit and had four chances to tie or take the lead in the final 30 seconds. The loss snapped Arizona's 12-game winning streak.

WILDCAT QUIZ

16. Prior to Lindsey's disastrous 1982-83 season, what was Arizona's worst record?

BRUIN WITH DISASTER The Wildcats never let up. The Trojans could attest to that. Before the Gumbies were inserted, Arizona built a 70-35 lead over USC before winning 92-48. It remains USC's worst league loss. Five Wildcats scored in double figures. Anthony Cook not only provided points, but 11 rebounds and four blocked shots.

Three days later UCLA thought it would clearly make a point — the West belongs to the Bruins.

Arizona trailed by two with six minutes remaining. The UA mounted a 22-8 run in the final minutes to record an 86-74 win.

Elliott again led the Wildcats with 27 points.

ARIZONA-BIG TEN CHAMPS First Michigan, then Iowa, then Michigan State. And to make a clean sweep, Arizona disposed of Illinois, 78-70, in front of a national television audience.

Tom Tolbert made 7 of 12 shots from the field to score 20 points, while Kerr made 6 of 8 field goals for 17.

NO. 1 IS A DANGEROUS PEDESTAL Again the AP ranked Arizona No. 1. Again, the Wildcats had to fight off a celebration mob after falling 82-74 to Stanford in Maples Pavilion. The "bouncy" floor in Palo Alto was doing a lot of shaking as the crowd hugged and partied, to the dismay of Wildcat players and coaches.

Even bigger news was the fact Kerr had two turnovers for the second game in a row.

PAULEY PAVILION — HOME AWAY FROM HOME For the second time in three years the Wildcats clinched the Pac-

10 title in Pauley Pavilion.

It took some doing this time. Arizona trailed UCLA, 73-71, before Elliott connected on a 15-foot jumper with three seconds left in regulation to send the game into overtime.

SCUM OF THE EARTH Many Arizona State fans displayed their true colors when, prior to the Wildcats' 101-73 victory over the Sun Devils in the regular season finale, chants of "Go back to Beirut" and "Where's your father" were directed at Kerr.

Kerr's father, Malcolm, was assassinated in Beirut in 1984.

"These people are the scum of the earth," Kerr said after the game.

Kerr got even by making his first seven shots from the field in the first half. The Sun Devil fans fired up the rest of the team as well. Arizona made 18-of-24 shots by halftime. Kerr finished with 22 points, five assists and zero turnovers.

PAC-10 DESTRUCTION The Pac-10 tournament was anti-climactic. The Wildcats not only were hosting the affair but had finished the regular season with a 17-1 mark.

There was no suspense:
California, 88-64.
Stanford, 97-83.
Oregon State, 93-67.

1987-88 RESULTS

Game	Result	Score	Margin	Game	Result	Score	Margin
Soviet Union	W	78-68	+10	Illinois	W	78-70	+8
Duquesne	W	133-78	+55	Stanford	L	82-74	-8
Michigan	W	79-64	+15	California	W	74-62	+12
Syracuse	W	80-69	+11	Oregon	W	89-57	+42
Long Beach State	W	94-62	+32	Oregon State	W	77-62	+15
Pepperdine	W	73-68	+5	USC	W	103-68	+35
Northern Arizona	W	77-59	+18	UCLA	W	78-76 ot	+2
Iowa	W	66-59	+7	Arizona State	W	101-73	+28
Arkansas-Little Rock	W	77-53	+24	Washington State	W	79-41	+28
Washington	W	110-71	+39	Washington	W	89-71	+18
Washington State	W	89-55	+34	**Pac-10 Tournament**			
Michigan State	W	78-58	+20	California	W	88-64	+24
Duke	W	91-85	+6	Stanford	W	97-83	+14
New Mexico	L	61-59	-2	Oregon State	W	93-67	+26
California	W	80-51	+29	**NCAA Tournament**			
Stanford	W	90-65	+25	Cornell	W	90-50	+40
Oregon State	W	70-48	+22	Seton Hall	W	84-55	+29
Oregon	W	70-54	+16	Iowa	W	99-79	+20
USC	W	92-48	+44	North Carolina	W	70-52	+18
UCLA	W	86-74	+12	**Final Four**			
Arizona State	W	99-59	+40	Oklahoma	L	86-78	-8

Elliott scored 20 points and had six assists in the victory over the Beavers. Cook added 19 points and eight rebounds. Arizona had won a Pac-10 record 31 games.

ROAD TO THE FINAL FOUR

POISON IVY The Wildcats made quick work of Ivy League champ Cornell, 90-50, to break its string of three-straight first-round losses. Cook had a career-high 24 points in the opening-round victory.

TOUGH GUYS Seton Hall was regarded as brutish. In contrast, the UA was considered soft despite constant battles against many of the country's more physical teams.

Arizona converted the non-believers.

The Wildcats built a 45-25 lead. Anthony Cook scored 20 points and Elliott contributed 19 in Arizona's 84-55 win.

SWEET 16 The first Iowa game was an emotional experience for everybody involved. The rematch was a disappointment — for Hawkeye fans.

Iowa relied on full-court pressure defense. Arizona countered with Kerr's fool-proof ball handling.

The Hawkeyes trimmed Arizona's lead to four at the half in the Seattle Kingdome. But the UA conducted a clinic on breaking the press, scoring 27 transition points. Arizona went 14 minutes without a turnover in the 99-79 win. Elliott led the Wildcats with 25 points and eight assists.

DEAN-O The last time the Wildcats had been one game away from reaching the Final Four, Fred Snowden's group faced UCLA in Pauley Pavilion. This time the odds were just as steep — so it seemed.

The obstacle was North Carolina and Dean Smith.

For just the second time all season Arizona trailed at halftime, 28-26. The Tar Heels, and all-American J.R. Reid, were formidable foes. But Reid was overshadowed in the second half by Arizona center Tom Tolbert. He made the play of a lifetime — a spinning throw-the-ball-behind-his-head-against-the-backboard-and-in shot.

"We play a lot of horse together and I teach him shots like that," Kerr said. "And Coach Olson just loves to see Tom up in the air throwing the ball over his head."

Tolbert scored 18 of his 21 points after intermission. Elliott finished with 24 points.

"To have the opportunity to reach the Final Four by defeating North Carolina, one of the very best programs in the country, and with one of the very best coaches in Dean Smith, made it even more special," Olson said.

Most UA Wins in a Season

Rank/Season	Wins
1. 1987-88	35
2. 1993-94	29
1988-89	29
4. 1990-91	28
5. 1995-96	26
6. 1989-90	25
1945-46	25
8. 1992-93	24
1991-92	24
1975-76	24
1949-50	24

Tom Tolbert's twisting, turning moves against North Carolina's J.R. Reid in the West Regional Finals proved too much to handle. Arizona's 80-62 win was the springboard to Kansas City and the Final Four.

TOLD YOU SO All those skeptics, including network sportscasters Brent Musberger and Billy Packer, had to eat their words following the 70-52 victory over North Carolina.

"We haven't been tested," Elliott went over and yelled to the national television audience, and especially to Musberger. "See you in the final game."

The celebration began on the court with the traditional net-cutting ceremony. Wilder antics took place in the locker room, where even Olson got his hair messed up.

"Sharing that with the guys on the team is the best thing that could have ever happened to me," Elliott said much later, after years in the NBA and participating in playoff and all-star games. "In the locker room after the North Carolina game, there was so much excitement. I had never seen so many guys excited. That is something that will never be duplicated."

FINAL FOUR Scalpers stood outside McKale Center with signs indicating tickets were available for Arizona's Final Four trip to Kansas City.

Thousand dollars a ticket. Thousand dollars a ticket.

Those lucky enough, or willing to empty the savings account, headed to Kansas City to cheer on a team that took every game seriously, while having fun in the process.

The Wildcats had beaten physical teams. Quicker teams. Well-coached teams.

"That was a run where nobody came close to us," Olson said. "That is unusual."

Still, Arizona heard the same criticism as Final Four opponent Oklahoma. Unproven. A surprise.

Yet, surprisingly, the Duke-Kansas game was considered the undercard. The Arizona-Oklahoma matchup looked to be for all the marbles.

DEJA VU In 1983 Iowa lost in the NCAA tournament while staying at the Alemeda Plaza Hotel in Kansas City — the same hotel Arizona was registered.

What's the significance? Well, it was at that hotel Arizona Athletic Director Cedric Dempsey first contacted Olson about the school's vacant coaching position. The next day they had breakfast for four hours, and, as they say, the rest is history.

Ironically, Olson's name surfaced again in a coaching search, this time at UCLA, following the departure of Walt Hazzard. "I'm not leaving," Olson said.

SOONERS BOOM The Sooners seemingly had all the answers. Stacey King and Harvey Grant controlled the paint. Mookie Blaylock and Ricky Grace provided the full-court press. That combination, along with Kerr's shooting nightmare, proved too much for Arizona to counter.

The Wildcats fell 86-78 despite Elliott's 31 points.

"They just beat us," Kerr said at the time. "They are a better basketball team."

That could still be debated. A normal Kerr game could have turned the tables; instead the Wildcat sharp-shooter was 2-of-13 from the field.

2-of-13.

There was a lot on Steve Kerr's mind the night he went 2-of-13 from the field against Oklahoma in the 1988 Final Four. Kerr made no excuses, but...

"His mother flew in from Egypt for that game. The only other game I remember he had a bad shooting game was against Stanford. He had family here that hardly ever came to the game. I don't know if that had any affect, but I think it added pressure. With Steve being such a perfectionist and so conscientious, I'm sure he wanted that to be his best game of his career. His mom. The Final Four. I think he put too much pressure on himself." — Coach Lute Olson, 1983-

"The biggest game of my life; it was the worst shooting night of my career," Kerr said. "I'm used to rising to the occasion. That is tough to take. That kills me."

Kerr missed more than three shots in a game on just three occasions all year.

KANSAS LUCKED OUT Years after the fact, Larry Brown, the head coach of the 1988 champion Jayhawks, was thankful Arizona hadn't gotten past Oklahoma.

"Larry Brown said he was praying they weren't going to play us," said Elliott, who played for Brown when he coached at San Antonio. "We felt we should have won it all."

Sean Elliott's 31 points against Oklahoma were not enough as Arizona's Cinderella season came to a close with an 86-78 setback at the hands of the Sooners.

Nearly 20,000 fans showed up at Arizona Stadium for a congratulations party despite the Final Four defeat. The players gave their thanks, danced, and sang in a good-time gathering for all. The team was escorted into the stadium with each player chauffeured in top-down convertibles.

WILDCATS ON PARADE A day after Kansas upset Oklahoma in the championship game, Arizona returned home to a hero's welcome.

Team members were paraded around the mall in convertibles, receiving royal treatment from more than 5,000 students, teachers, administrators, and fans.

The convertible convoy converged on Arizona Stadium, where more than 15,000 fans waited in the hot sun. Little did they know that the contingent was late because the team stopped at Der Weinerschnitzel for something to eat.

A little mustard, please.

School was called off for anyone who wanted to attend the celebration.

"You guys will do anything to get out of class, won't you," Olson said with a laugh.

The fans were not in the stands to get out of an algebra test. They were there to honor a team that earned the No. 1 ranking in the country, won the Pac-10 title (with a 17-1 record), appeared in the school's first Final Four, and became synonymous with "team basketball."

"Not very many players have accomplished the things we did," Tolbert said.

THE 1993-94 SEASON — ANOTHER FINAL FOUR

Sticks and stones can hurt, but so can names.

Throughout the 1993-94 season those affiliated with the Arizona basketball program were convinced others thought of them as "chokers" and "losers" after NCAA Tournament first-round defeats in 1992 and 1993.

"Everybody was finding negative things to write and talk about," Olson recalls. "The players are just like the staff. We get sick and tired of the negative talk. There are a lot of negative people out there, but we know there is a large silent majority that is very supportive of this program. Unfortunately, we don't hear as much from the silent majority. That was a motivator and a tremendous amount of pressure to deal with."

That and the fact that Chris Mills, the 1993 Pac-10 Player of the Year, and big guy Ed Stokes were no longer on the roster. This made for a different makeup. This transformed Olson from a coach who preferred to have a big guy down low controlling the action.

Olson called for Damon Stoudamire and Khalid Reeves to take the ball with a no holds barred approach. They did just that — all the way to the Final Four in Charlotte.

The "En Garde" tandem, featured in fencing outfits on the cover of the 1994 Arizona basketball media guide, was devastating. Reeves and Stoudamire accounted for high-scoring honors in all but two games.

Reeves, who would later be a first-round pick of the Miami Heat, averaged 24.2 points per game, a single-season scoring record, and compiled 848 points, becoming the only player in school history to top Sean Elliott's 743.

Before Reeves' act concluded in the Charlotte Arena,

For years, every player, team, and coach had lived under the expectations set down by the 1988 team. The burden was too much for others, but not the 1993-94 team, which went to Charlotte for Arizona's second NCAA Final Four appearance.

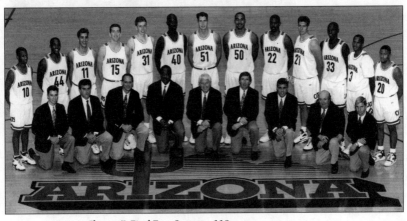

he owned single-season records in scoring average, field goals made, field goals attempted, and free throws made and attempted.

Stoudamire showed Kerr-esque perimeter range to compile 18.3 points an outing and 208 assists.

"What stands out was the play of those two guards," Olson said. "There were some games when they both were on, which meant the total destruction of some people. What helped is that if Khalid didn't have a great game, Damon would and vice versa. It was the ability for one guy to pick up the other if one wasn't on their game."

DOWN UNDER The Wildcats went on a working vacation to answer many of the questions surrounding the program. Not only were there questions about the first-round losses, but doubts about a front line that no longer had the height afforded by Sean Rooks, Ed Stokes, and Brian Williams, even Mills.

Arizona was a smaller but faster team for the first time since Olson's early years in Tucson.

The collection of talent went to Australia for a 10-game tour that became a prelude of things to come.

Arizona posted a 9-1 record, but more impressively, registered triple-digit point outcomes in all but one

The season started with a three-week journey to Australia and a 10-game exhibition tour. Along with nine wins the Wildcats' Joseph Blair and Reggie Geary did some scuba diving.

matchup. Arizona surpassed the 120-point barrier five times.

The new style was working.

"What I thought was the key to the 1994 season was the trip we took to Australia," Olson said. "Spending three weeks on the road together really brought everyone together."

AUSTRALIAN TOUR STATS

Player	Pts	Reb	Assists
Khalid Reeves	25.8	4.4	35
Damon Stoudamire	18.9	2.5	55
Ray Owes	12.2	9.5	2
Joe McLean	11.3	3.8	17
Joseph Blair	10.1	7.3	4
Dylan Rigdon	8.6	2.3	24
Corey Williams	8.5	4.6	8
Etdrick Bohannon	8.0	8.9	2
Reggie Geary	6.8	2.9	28
Kevin Flanagan	5.7	4.4	9

17. What prominent member of the NCAA was an assistant coach for Bruce Larson and was the school's freshman coach during the 1965-66 season?

There was plenty of sun and fun visiting the Great Barrier Reef and the Gold Coast, taking harbor cruises, touring zoos, and looking over Perth, Adelaide, Melbourne, Auckland, Brisbane, and Cairns.

"When we were away from the court, it was a vacation," Arizona assistant coach Jessie Evans said. "As soon as the games or practices took place, it was work."

Reeves tried to learn to swim: "I had pushed him in my pool, so I knew he was afraid of the water, but here he was in the Great Barrier Reef trying to snorkel," Evans said. "He had his life jacket on. I couldn't believe it."

Kevin Flanagan and Dylan Rigdon, when they weren't surfing, were off bungee jumping.

Eating was a problem for many: "A lot of us didn't like the food," Corey Williams said. "I think I ate McDonald's for 20 days."

Where's mom when she is needed? The players had to take care of their own laundry, including game uniforms. Ray Owes wound up putting his red and white uniforms together. The final product was pink. Others neglected some of their responsibilities.

"(McLean's) jersey once was so dirty that right before a game they were trying to find an alternate," Williams said. "And I won't say any names, but I think there were a couple of guys who didn't wash their uniforms at all. It was pretty obvious."

ODD COUPLE Stoudamire could tell you who was on the roster of the 1945 Cincinnati Royals. He's also the one who would iron his socks before going out on the town.

Khalid Reeves and Damon Stoudamire lived up to their marquee billing in 1994.

Reeves could hardly tell you who the next opponent would be and would hang out by himself.

They weren't exactly a perfect match, but as roommates, a backcourt combination, and friends, they made for a lethal combination.

"They became very good friends," Olson said. "That helped both of them grow to where two people can be totally different in the way they were and the way they think, but it shows you can still be really good friends."

THERE IS A FRONT LINE, TOO Reeves and Stoudamire could run and shoot, but somebody had to rebound and provide scoring in the paint. Ray Owes and Joseph Blair answered the call.

The first proof came against "Big Country" Bryant Reeves and his Oklahoma State Cowboys. The 7-footer was expected to handle the Wildcats inside. The reverse occurred as Owes made 7 of 12 shots and scored 16 points, while Blair came off the bench to tally 14 points. Final score: UA 97, OSU 84.

Reeves was a non-factor with 12 points and six

rebounds.

"That front line made unbelievable strides that year," Olson said. "They got slighted at times because of the guards. Ray Owes became a really, really solid player. JB became a factor for us board-wise and defensively."

ALOHA In the blink of an eye Arizona went from winning the Maui Classic to a buzzer-beating defeat in the championship game.

After Reeves led Arizona with 32 points in a 98-79 victory over Notre Dame, and Reggie Geary hit crucial three-pointers in a 70-65 win over Boston College, the Wildcats took on No. 5 ranked Kentucky for the championship trophy.

With an ESPN audience looking on, the two Wildcat teams played "a classic."

Arizona rallied from an 11-point deficit in the first half to take a 79-78 lead with 6:25 remaining. With the lead changing every time an all-American play was made, the outcome remained in doubt.

Two free throws by Reeves with 5.5 seconds left gave Arizona a one-point lead, but a Kentucky desperation shot was tipped in at the buzzer by Jeff Brassow for a 93-92 UK win.

The 1994 Wildcats had a universe of high hopes and accomplishments of near equal proportions.

Kentucky won the game, but Arizona won the battle of premier backcourt tandems with Reeves scoring 31 and Stoudamire 28. Kentucky's Travis Ford had 25, while Tony Delk added 18.

"Kentucky was obviously one of the most talented teams in the country, if not the most talented," Olson said. "The fact on a neutral court we played them that tough and actually had the game won was an indication that yes, we knew we were good. If we were in a position to beat Kentucky, then we have a chance to be very, very good."

TALK IS CHEAP Michigan players walked off the McKale Center floor after the championship game of the Fiesta Bowl Classic without the traditional handshake.

Losing 119-95 can make bad losers out of some.

"Michigan has no class, no class whatsoever," Geary said. "They were taking cheap shots, not wanting to shake our hands. It was a hard-fought battle. The least they could do is come over and shake our hands. If they can't do that, then we know what they are made of."

The Wolverines found no avenue to stop Reeves, the tournament's MVP. The Wildcat guard scored 40 points, making 13 of 14 field goals and 11-of-12 free throws. Reeves was 10 of 11 against Fordham from the field in the opening game.

"He hurt us," Michigan's Juwan Howard said. "He was hot. We tried to contain him, but he was unstoppable."

REUNION Kevin O'Neill spent years recruiting players just like Stoudamire and Reeves to Arizona. Upon his return to Tucson his Marquette team had to face the tandem, and the Warriors lost 94-80.

Some of O'Neill's comments:
■ "They are like a stun gun. I felt we got hit by a stun gun halfway through the first half."
■ "Those two guards ... not since (Walt) Frazier and (Earl) Monroe have there been two guards like those guys."
■ "It almost seems like a H-O-R-S-E game with those two guys. Over the rim, off the backboard, off Coach O'Neill's head, through Wilbur the Wildcat's legs, and no rim. It's a joke. Those two guys are really good."
■ "(Craig) McMillan was down here scouting the Michigan game. He called me at home after the game. I said, 'Mac, are they as quick in person as they are on TV?' He said they are a lot quicker in person. I was really excited about that. ... It was just awful."
■ "I know how a lot of people used to feel when I was sitting on the other bench and the score was 40-20 or 60-20."

WILDCAT QUIZ

18. By virtue of the number of points they scored as freshmen, what class ranks the best all time at Arizona?

RUNNING THE TABLE At the midway point of the Pac-10 season the Wildcats were 6-3, in third place, two games behind UCLA. Losses to California at McKale, which snapped a 21-game home winning streak, at UCLA, and an embarrassing setback at Washington, put winning a fifth title in six years in serious jeopardy.

"In order to have a chance to defend the Pac-10 title we need to run the table and get a little help from some other schools," Olson told the team following the loss in Seattle.

The table scraps included Stanford (77-60 losers), California (96-77), USC (94-61), UCLA (98-74), Oregon State (96-69), Oregon (75-71), Washington (95-62), and Washington State (85-69).

Except for a 94-87 loss in Tempe to end the regular season, the Wildcats had done what Olson had asked and other schools had helped. UCLA and California both lost on the same day, giving Arizona the league championship.

After back-to-back first-round losses, all eyes were on the Wildcats. Would they fall again? Loyola (Md.) was no match in the opening game of the tournament as Arizona prevailed 81-55.

CHOKE FACTOR "This is not a choking team," Geary said. "That is ridiculous."

Questions were numerous, all relating to disappointing past NCAA Tournament losses to East Tennessee State and Santa Clara.

"We are not thinking about the loss to Santa Clara other than using it for motivation to get us going," Kevin Flanagan said.

If the Wildcats needed an additional reminder of what can happen in a first-round game, Tulsa provided it when the Hurricane eliminated UCLA.

Arizona made certain Loyola (Md.) would not become a household name as McLean came off the bench to score six points to spark a 16-0 run midway through the first half.

"We proved a lot of people wrong," Blair said. "A lot of people thought we would lose the first-round game."

Virginia's Cornell Parker was expected to shut down Khalid Reeves, who found himself in "a shooting zone" during the tournament. Parker was not up to the task and neither were the Cavaliers as Arizona prevailed 71-58 to reach the Sweet 16. In the initial four tournament games the senior guard scored 32, 30, 29, and 26 points.

SWEET 16 BOUND Virginia was said to be more physical and the Cavaliers also had Cornell Parker — whom Dick Vitale had declared the country's best defensive player — to offset Reeves.

What does Vitale know anyway?

Reeves scored 30 points in Arizona's 71-58 victory. As for the more physical aspect, Blair had 12 rebounds and Owes 15 points and 10 boards.

FINAL FOUR TREATMENT Blair went to Los Angeles with two things in mind: getting Arizona to the Final Four and to make a name for himself against Louisville's Clifford Rozier in the round of 16.

Blair 12 points, 10 rebounds. Rozier—five points.

Arizona 82, Louisville 70.

In the West Regional championship at the Sports Arena in Los Angeles the Wildcats faced No. 1 seed Missouri, which had gone 14-0 in Big 8 play. It was expected to be a challenge.

Arizona was up to the call with Stoudamire and Reeves battling for game-high scoring honors. Stoudamire won with 27, one more than Reeves in the Wildcats' 92-72 victory.

"We are not only beating people, we have been

With a definite home crowd on its side, Arizona traveled to the Sports Arena in Los Angeles to take on Louisville, a team analysts said had the best starting five in the country, including highly touted big man Clifford Rozier. Arizona rolled to an 82-70 win.

blowing them out," Stoudamire said afterward. "Coach came into the locker room and said this reminds him of the 1988 Final Four team when they were blowing people out."

IN A LEAGUE OF HIS OWN There was no player better than Reeves after the first four games of the tournament.

Following the 92-72 domination of No. 1 seed Missouri in the West Region Final, Damon Stoudamire discussed the Wildcats' chances with Dick Stockton and Al McGuire.

Despite harassing defenses, changing looks, defensive "specialists," and slow-down tactics, Reeves had scored 32 against Loyola, 30 against Virginia, 29 against Louisville, and 26 against Missouri.

Yet, Reeves said he had not hit the "shooting zone."

"When I'm in a zone, I make most of my shots," Reeves said. "Everything is going well."

"I can understand him saying he is not in a zone," Corey Williams said. "When people are in a zone, they aren't thinking anymore. I've seen Khalid in a zone. If Khalid is ever to get in a zone it would be quite absurd."

THE FINAL FOUR-CHARLOTTE

"There is more in store at the Final Four."

These words were written on the chalkboard after Arizona's victory over Missouri. Unlike the 1988 team, which had some players admit to being happy just to get there, this team wanted — no, expected — to win the national championship.

And they were plenty irritated with the labels hung on them.

"I'm tremendously proud of this group of guys who have been dubbed and questioned and called chokers and losers," Olson said to the national media. Olson took every opportunity to express his displeasure with the media for its often harsh treatment of a top 10 program.

Hard feelings developed, but the Wildcats turned that into motivation.

"I don't want three teams ahead of me saying they are better than we are," Blair said. "I'm going to Charlotte to win."

PRESIDENT CLINTON Arkansas' First Fan was in the house to watch the Razorbacks win the national championship.

Extra security was needed. Metal detectors were set up at all entrances. Searches of purses and media bags were mandatory, resulting in long lines to get into the Charlotte Coliseum.

Arizona's sharpshooting guards missed their mark, and despite an excellent effort by Ray Owes (22) the UA fell 91-82 to Arkansas, which won the national title two days later.

COLD SHOOTING Reeves was six of 19 against Arkansas. Stoudamire was five of 24. Ray Owes managed to keep Arizona within striking distance with 16 points and 12 rebounds.

Despite not finding the range often, Stoudamire's near-halfcourt shot at the half-time buzzer closed a once 12-point Arkansas lead to three. By the time Williams came off the bench to connect on back-to-back three-pointers Arizona had a 57-52 lead.

Reeves' fourth foul, Corey Beck's Kerr-like ability to steady the Arkansas offense, and Corliss Williamson's 29 points eventually overcame the Wildcats.

WELCOME HOME PARTY Just as in 1988 a welcoming ceremony was organized. About 8,000 fans occupied Arizona Stadium to cheer on the 1994 Wildcats one last time.

STOP THE COMPARISONS For years, each and every Wildcat player received the benefit and the luggage placed on them by the success of the 1988 Wildcats, regarded as the best team in Arizona history.

The 1994 cast members felt it was time to look at Reeves and Stoudamire and not Kerr and McMillan. Look at Ray Owes, Joseph Blair and Reggie Geary instead of Elliott, Cook and Tolbert.

"We've been living in the shadow of the 1988 team. Every team has been trying to out-do them, but this year people will look back and say these guys played well together, they played a completely new style of ball and I think the fans really enjoyed it, as well as the players," Dylan Rigdon said.

So, will a 29-6 record, a Final Four appearance and

CATS IN THE NBA

Wildcats drafted by NBA teams

Year	Rnd/No.	Player	Team
1996	2nd/35	Joseph Blair	Seattle
1996	2nd/43	Ben Davis	Phoenix
1996	2nd/56	Reggie Geary	Cleveland
1995	1st/7	Damon Stoudamire	Toronto
1994	1st/12	Khalid Reeves	Miami
1993	1st/22	Chris Mills	Cleveland
1993	2nd/35	Ed Stokes	Miami
1992	2nd/30	Sean Rooks	Dallas
1991	1st/10	Brian Williams	Orlando
1990	2nd/38	Jud Buechler	Seattle
1989	1st/3	Sean Elliott	San Antonio
1989	1st/24	Anthony Cook	Phoenix
1988	2nd/34	Tom Tolbert	Charlotte
1988	2nd/50	Steve Kerr	Phoenix
1985	4th/89	Pete Williams	Denver
1985	7th/158	Eddie Smith	Denver
1984	1st/10	Leon Wood	Philadelphia
1983	8th/177	Frank Smith	Portland
1981	4th/177	Ron Davis	Washington
1981	7th/148	Robbie Dosty	Golden State
1981	10th	Phil Tayor	Denver
1980	7th	Joe Nehls	Houston
1979	1st/9	Larry Demic	N.Y. Knicks
1977	2nd/42	Bob Elliott	Philadelphia
1977	2nd	Herman Harris	Philadelphia
1976	2nd/30	Al Fleming	Seattle
1976	5th	Jim Rappis	Milwaukee
1974	2nd/33	Eric Money	Detroit
1974	3rd/35	Coniel Norman	Philadelphia
1968	12th	Bill Davis	Phoenix
1965	4th	Warren Rustand	Golden State
1948	-	Morris Udall	Denver

Reggie Geary and Joseph Blair show off their Final Four hardware at a celebration in Arizona Stadium.

another Pac-10 title be good enough to erase past success — and failures?

"I don't know how people will look back at this team," Geary said. "That will be judged five years from now. We know we have made ourselves proud, our parents proud and Tucson proud."

A Sunny Future in Store

Even in the foundling days of Wildcat basketball, recruiting was the key component to success.

During the Fred Enke era, the base of players in Tucson and Phoenix was more than enough to compete with foes from the Border Conference. But wins in the WAC and later the Pac-10 came a lot tougher without the best players available.

Larson struggled through the WAC years with virtually no recruiting base and a worn-out gymnasium. Fred Snowden discovered initial success by taking talent from the snow-belt of Michigan, Wisconsin and Indiana. And then Snowden felt there were enough players out West to compete with the UCLAs.

Lute Olson has received much hardware throughout his coaching career. He strives for that elusive national championship before his retirement, possibly in 2000.

Mike Bibby heads an all-star 1996 recruiting class that also features Stephen Jackson, Bennett Davison, Eugene Edgerson, Quynn Tebbs, and Justin Wessel.

The players are out there, but they must sign on the dotted lines. That became a tremendous obstacle. It was not until Lute Olson arrived in Tucson that California became a prime recruiting area. Sure, he received the homegrown talents of Sean Elliott, but with the exception of just one or two others, Olson and his assistants wore out their luggage by leaving the Grand Canyon State for greener pastures.

Los Angeles, Seattle, New York, Houston, the high profile cities, have become bases to which Olson travels. The recent No. 1 recruiting class signifies the progress Arizona has made.

Olson is the first to tell you that staying competitive in the recruiting game is not easy, with the larger markets having built-in NCAA rule advantages. Just the same, Mike Bibby, Stephen Jackson, Eugene Edgerson, Bennett Davison, Quynn Tebbs, and Justin Wessel all will play in the Old Pueblo with the future of the program securely in their hands.

Olson has brought success, maintained it, and looks for even higher plateaus down the road. The silver-haired gentleman has a contract through 2000.

What then?

"I will continue what I'm doing as long as I enjoy it and as long as I'm effective at what I'm doing and as long as I have the energy," Olson said.

After that, somebody else will have to step in, just like Enke did, and Larson, and Snowden.

Will the heir apparent duplicate the amount of victories, take the team to the Final Four or win a national championship? Nobody hopes so more than Olson himself.

Eugene Edgerson

"When I came here, the point I was trying to make is that we were not interested in building a team as much as we are a program," Olson said. "That is the test of a basketball program. It is how efficient you can stay, not if you are winning a national title every year or getting to the Final Four. It's a matter of not having a down year. A down year might be finishing second in the conference race and winning only 24 games.

"Once I leave, we hope we built a program on firm foundation that will continue to be successful. From my standpoint, I hope it is more successful than during the time that I've been here. That will be the test."

NO. 1 RECRUITING CLASS Helping to keep a smile on Olson's face is a 1996 recruiting class ranked No. 1 in the nation by several recruiting services.

The centerpiece is Mike Bibby, the country's top-rated point guard, from Shadow Mountain High School in Phoenix. With Bibby handling the ball the Wildcats appear to be set — as long as he remains.

"I think he is one of the top point guards I have watched throughout the years," Olson said. "He has an uncanny ability to find the open man. It is not only getting the ball to someone, it's getting the ball to somebody at the right place at the right time. His ability to see the floor and his timing of his passes are really something."

And Bibby might not even be the best player recruited. Forward Stephen Jackson is a top 15 player as well. Edgerson is a top 25 player.

Wins in the future? Yeah, they are likely.

Memories

The following are key moments or thoughts from those closely involved in Arizona basketball for several decades:

JUST SAY "YES" "There are some guys who flat-out cannot say no. Sean Elliott is one of the all-time guys who was like that. He never said, 'No.' There was one time I spoke to the TUSD teachers and administrators. I don't know how many people came up to me and said 'Sean did such a good job of talking to our kids.' I was hearing this over and over and over again. I came back to the office and checked to see how many places we sent Sean. It was a case of Sean doing these things on his own from the requests of teachers instead of saying you have to call the basketball office. That probably tells you more about Sean than anything. He is somebody who loves kids and is somebody who grew up in the community and knew the importance of being a role model."
— *Coach Lute Olson, 1983-*

Sean Elliott (32) spoke to children at Tucson elementary schools on a regular basis.

TOM TOLBERT-ALWAYS SOMETHING TO SAY The media loves to head into a locker room to get the "good quote." Steve Kerr was always accommodating, but the guy most everybody loved on that 1988 squad was Tom Tolbert, Arizona's charismatic center.

Nobody ever knew what practical joke would be invented or what comments would come from the King of the Zingers.

The mystery is part of the legend.

■ "I can't tell any of Tolbert's jokes without turning Lute's face red," Sean Elliott said.

■ "Is this an X-rated book? I don't think there are any stories I can tell about him," Craig McMillan indicated.

Tom Tolbert never lacked for words.

That was the general theme. Ask Tolbert about some of his former teammates and there is little hesitation:

Sean Elliott — "Sean was a classic. He drove his car like he was playing a video game. We would go up to the foothills and he would be zooming around like he just put a quarter into the machine. I told him this isn't a game and he yelled, 'Yahoo.' Sean loved to drive in the foothills. He didn't drive dangerously. He was fairly cautious, but he did love to put his foot on the pedal."

Steve Kerr — "It was Halloween night our senior year. We were going to this party. We had already had a few beers. We go to this frat party, I think. We asked the guy in front how we get in here. He said you have to wear a costume. Steve and I didn't have a costume. We went back to Steve's place to get more beer. We see these empty 12-pack containers. We decided to put them on our heads and walk back over there. The guy asked us what we are. I told him we are a 12-pack, but together we are a case. They let us in."

Craig McMillan — "We were roommates at Babcock Hall. We were two totally different people with different likes. He loved our apartment as hot as you could get it. I loved it cold. It was a constant battle — from him turning the heat on, me the AC. Heat. AC. Heat. AC. One night I woke up and it was 125 degrees in the room. I thought I was in Ecuador. My mouth was so dry. I had to crawl to the thermometer. Ferns were growing out of my sneakers. Craig's in the bathroom. I won't even tell you what the smell was like. It was like a Jaws movie. Finally to keep it cool, I broke the button off after turning the AC on and told Craig to try to turn the heat back on now."

Bruce Fraser — "We got rid of Bruce for my senior year. That was special and probably better for us."

Anthony Cook — "We would work in the summers to earn some money. One year we got a job working with asphalt on a road crew. It was good money. We worked our butts off from 6 in the morning until 6 at night. I did it for a week. I quit. AC wanted to get money, wanted money to goose up his car. He was amazing. I stayed two days and said, 'Only three more days of this for me.' AC stayed there working for nine weeks. He was crazy."

Gumbies — "These guys were abused in practice. They went to practice and were abused by us. They never complained though, and always worked hard. They became the best part of the team. They would go nuts in the games."

Kevin O'Neill — "You could always tell him what was on your mind and he would tell you what was on his mind as well. He was a fiery personality, just like me. There were never any repercussions when you called him an a—hole as long as you worked your butt off 30 minutes later. But, boy there was never anybody who wanted to win more than him."

Lute Olson — "He couldn't have taken me for four years. Two was enough. His hair went from grey to white just in that time. If I would have been there four years he would have went bald. I don't think that is a good look for him."

On the 1988 team — "Everybody was always saying this team did not have a lot of talent, that we only had good chemistry and a good cohesiveness, but we also had a lot of talent. I guess excuses were needed for all the ass kickings."

His own practical jokes — "I don't remember them. I'm usually in an illusionary state."

Going to class — "Something has to be done about that going to class thing. Going to class really puts a damper on things."

Yet, there is no joking around when he discusses his 21-point performance and personal battle with North Carolina's J.R. Reid in the Western Regional Finals in 1988.

"That is the most remembered game of my career. The significance of it. It wasn't just another game. I started out poorly. By the time it was over, I helped us get to the Final Four. To do it against J.R. Reid and North Carolina with Dean Smith was pretty special. I still have the player of the game plaque. I look at it and remember all the good memories."

BAIL ME OUT LUTE! At the 1989 NCAA tournament in Boise, Idaho, Arizona assistant coach Kevin O'Neill and several boosters tested the city night life:

"Me, Burt Kinerk and Bob Mueller went out for St. Patrick's Day after scouting the Clemson game. It's late at night, I've been in my room all day scouting so we decided, 'All right, we'll sneak out for a couple of beers.' Well, we get blitzed.

"We nearly get in a fight in the bar with a guy who's

WILDCAT QUIZ

19. Name the only player Lute Olson tried to recruit who was on Ben Lindsey's team.

calling Lute an a—hole and he's wearing these green garters on both arms and a green glow-in-the-dark headband. I'm ready, let's fight if you're going to be dressed up. We wind up going back to the hotel and Kinerk and me and Craig McMillan are loud. We're carrying on and I'm in my room and the police come in the room, throw me against the wall and put me in cuffs.

"Now I'm going to the police station. I call Lute. I tell Lute they're taking me down. He sends (George) Kalil and (Steve) Condon down to get me. I tell you what, that was a long night. I'm in some glass cage thing with an open toilet and there were about 40 guys (relieving themselves) all over the place. I got out just in time for the game.

"I've got just enough time to go on a jog with (*Tucson Citizen* columnist) Corky (Simpson). We go for a jog and then come back for the pregame meal. Of course Lute knows about it, but he doesn't say anything. As we're getting ready to go on the bus, he walks by me and says, 'You'd better hope we win.' At halftime we were down. I told Sean (Elliott), whatever you do, you'd better make sure we win this game or my ass is grass." — Kevin O'Neill, Arizona assistant coach from 1986-89 and current Tennessee head coach.

One of the most flamboyant personalities in UA basketball lore was also one of the most successful and well-thought-of assistant coaches — Kevin O'Neill.

RECRUITING GUMBIES "They probably got as much attention drawn to the program as the starters did. I remember going into homes that spring in recruiting. The parents wanted to talk about the Gumbies. What it pointed out was that this was not just a team that had starters happy, this was a program that everybody supported. They were very influential in our future recruiting." — *Lute Olson.*

THE LONGEST DAY "We started calling this trip to Oregon — the longggestt day. We left early in the morning to get there. We had to go to San Francisco, change planes and go to Portland and then bus to Eugene, but our flight got delayed for four or five hours. It took all day to get to Portland. Then we had to bus an hour and a half to Eugene.

"We started this thing called — the looonngggest day. Somebody would start a story like on February whatever, Harvey Mason was seen walking through the terminal in Tucson and was never heard from again. And then everybody in the bus would yell — the lonngggesst day. It was like a chant.

"We all had a little story. On this day, Sean Elliott woke up, kissed his mother good-bye, got a hamburger or a burrito at the airport and has never been heard from again. And the bus would go — the loonngggest day."— —*Sean Elliott, 1986-89.*

Ricky Byrdsong is called for a foul — with Lute taking the charge.

TAKE THAT LUTE "There was the time Lute tried to take a charge from Coach (Ricky) Byrdsong. They fell all over each other like clowns. The whole team wanted to laugh, but we didn't because we didn't want to run all day. It was pretty funny. Byrd just ran right over him. The ball was rolling away. They were on the floor all tangled up over each other. Lute fell right on his butt."
— *Sean Elliott, 1986-89.*

PARTY HARD "We just finished losing three straight games at the Kentucky Invitational Tournament. We were going to Murray State to play. It was a dry county. A bunch of us decided we have to have a drink for New Year's. We went to Paris, Tennessee. We were supposed to be in at midnight. The guy who was driving had one finger on the wheel and was going about 100 miles per hour.

"It was about 3:30 in the morning when we got back. Fred (Enke) was outside pacing. We honked when we got up to him, waved, and then went into town to get something to eat. Our punishment was having to run two extra laps. Everybody started the game. There were three or four starters in the car." — *Bob Mueller, 1956-58.*

GET YOUR OWN RIDE HOME "Playing Ole Miss in the Memphis Classic we were down big at halftime and Fred (Enke) is in the locker room at halftime beside himself. He is lacerating us all — as he should. With 28 seconds to play we were down by one. Fred didn't stand up long, but he was kneeling almost the whole second half.

"We're coming down the court when Allan Stanton goes down. He hurt his right knee. He has some ligament damage and the ball goes out of bounds. Fred gets all mad. I had never seen him jump so high before. He's yelling at Allan, who is lying there with his thigh forward and his right calf, lower leg going the other direction. We ended up losing (75-70). When we got into the locker room Fred told us we played a good second half, but to find our own way back to the hotel. We had to either walk, pay for a cab out of our own money, or find another way. It was the only time that happened." — *George Rountree, 1953-55.*

BOMBS AWAY "We always ate at 4 p.m., no matter what. It didn't matter if the game started at 7 or 8 or 10. We always ate at 4 o'clock and we ate the same food every time. It was well-cooked roast beef, baked potato without butter or sour cream, toast, jelly, and a salad with French dressing. It had to be French dressing, if you liked French dressing or not.

"After dinner we could go for a walk, get a nap before game time. There was one time I went to my room on the eighth floor. I opened up the window and saw Fred (Enke) walking down on the sidewalk. I threw a cherry bomb. It went off about 10 feet behind him. I wasn't trying to hit him. I turned around and hid under the bed covers when Fred was knocking at the door to let him in. My roommate, James Brower, opened the door timidly and Fred comes in and said 'You did that, didn't you?' I told him I was just trying to take a nap. He said 'You threw that firecracker at me.' I told him you don't need a firecracker to set you off." — *George Rountree, 1953-55*

WORKING SCHOLARSHIP "A scholarship in those days is not like it is now. You were a linen boy at the dorm. You handed out linen once a week to change the beds. I had to work at the student union to earn my food. I had to work at the football games. I ran the scoreboard, 10-0 and first and 10. We always screwed that up. The ball would be at the 3 yard line and we would have it at the 10. It was a beat up old scoreboard. Books were included." — *Bill Reeves, 1955-57.*

FOUL SEASON "My fouls were higher than my scoring average at times. I got six fouls once. The guy forgot to whistle me out. I knew I had five fouls, but I just kept playing. I got my sixth and then finally they sat me down. ... (I got so many fouls) because, to be honest, without me the guys wouldn't cover their men very well and their guys would drive in and they would say, 'Take him Reeves.' I'm not very coordinated, but I thought I made some pretty good blocks. I had some long arms. I could block shots. They didn't keep blocked shots. A foul in those days was like a tap on the arm. It was awful. I would hit the ball and they would call a foul on me."
— *Bill Reeves, 1955-57.*

ORANGE YOU GLAD THEY MISSED "We were in Texas, I believe playing Hardin-Simmons. They gave every fan

Joe Skaisgir could also play D.

who came into the building an orange. For what reason I don't know. I do know what they used them for. One of our guards stole the ball and went for a layup when somebody threw an orange and it hit the backboard. It startled him and he missed the layup. Then another time, Bruce Larson stood up to complain about something and Fred (Enke) grabs him and says, 'Sit down, you are due for an orange.'" — *Joe Skaisgir, 1960-61.*

THAT'S HOW TO PLAY DEFENSE "We were playing UCLA. Art LaZar was guarding this guy (Gary) Cunningham, who had hit seven straight shots. They were long shots. There was no stopping him. Fred says to Art, 'we are going to put Joe on him.' The first time down the court he puts a shot up. It was way out of even his range. I had no chance of stopping him. The ball came just short. It rolled off. Fred goes over to Art and says, 'See Art, that is how you do it.' Fred was the type of coach who could always come up with a funny line." — *Joe Skaisgir, 1960-61.*

KERR QUIRKS The following are a few comments from and about Steve Kerr during his UA career:
■ "Kerr can be warrior-like, as irrepressible as a tornado and loquacious as Dick Vitale and as perfect a role model

Steve Kerr is (25) now in the NBA. One day he might be Tucson's Mayor.

as that legendary all-American boy Jack Armstrong." — *Chicago Tribune.*

■ "Frankly, they wouldn't recruit me now, and Coach Olson would tell you that. I just wasn't that good." — *Kerr in 1988 about his status coming out of high school.*

■ "He could probably run for mayor of Tucson and win." — *former USC Coach George Raveling.*

■ "He's like a coach on the floor, but he has more physical ability than Lute." — *Sean Elliott*

■ "If Steve said green was yellow, the staff and the team would be there nodding their heads yes. That's the kind of hold he has over the people in the program." — *Lute Olson*

■ "Kerr, an unlikely star who appears to have materialized from the script of an Andy Hardy movie, to the Wildcat playmaker, clutch shot maker and faith healer." — *Chicago Tribune.*

■ "I'm going back to Tucson, get Lute fired and take over his job." — *Kerr after his knee injury at the World Championships in Spain.*

HOW TALL ARE YOU AGAIN? "Freddy's (Snowden) heights were never correct. Now the controversy is that everybody is finding out Ben Davis is 6-6 3/4. I was listed at 6-10. I am not 6-10 yet. They must have been counting some of that Afro I had. There is no way I was 6-10. Actually that hurt me when I went to the Olympic Trials. They put me down, Bob Elliott as 6-10, 230 from Arizona. I get up there and the first thing they do is take your shoes off and put you up against the wall. John Thompson, the coach there, parts my afro and puts a stick on my head and says I'm 6-8 1/4. Then he makes me move, tells me to get out of there, come back in a couple of minutes. We just beat them. You can't be 6-8 1/4 he says. There is no way. I say take a look again. The truth was out." — *Bob Elliott, 1973-77.*

LAST ONE IN IS A ROTTEN EGG "A couple of years ago when Sean (Elliott) got married, Coach Olson threw a party for the guys from our days out at his house. The night of the rehearsal we went over there. We all ended up in the pool with all of our clothes on. Before that I leaned over to Matt (Muehlebach) and asked him if he would go into the pool with all his clothes on. That is something you just wouldn't do, not at Coach Olson's house. We have way too much respect to do something like that at Coach Olson's house, but Matt said he would if Steve (Kerr) does. I went over to Steve and asked him the same thing. Steve said 'I will if you will.' So we all jumped in. Steve, (Tom) Tolbert, Muehlebach, (Steve) Condon (the team's trainer back then) were in the pool with really nice

clothes on. Coach Olson loved it. He was running around taking care of us. Coach Olson eventually jumped in. He had gone to put on shorts, but he had his shirt on. That was a huge thing for all of us. He was one of us and not just our coach. It was the first time we all looked at him that way. It was good. He sat in the Jacuzzi with us talking and laughing about all the good stories. We were also getting on him for getting his hair wet."
— *Bruce Fraser, 1985-87*.

MACHETE MADNESS "In my freshman year in El Paso, this fool kept walking behind the bench with a trenchcoat and kept opening it up and he had a machete. He kept saying 'I have something for you guys when the game is over, I've got something for you guys.' With a minute left we are up by six. Freddie says, 'We know we have the fool here, make sure you are up by at least four with five seconds to go because with five seconds left and if we are up by four we are going to take off running.' We were up. We gave them the last basket. It made no difference. We were out of there." — *Bob Elliott, 1973-77*.

MILE-HIGH CLUB "We were flying from Laramie on an old Frontier Airline, everybody was afraid to get on one of those, when the emergency door cracked open. You could see an inch of space. It was about 20 degrees, the wind was blowing and the plane was bouncing all around. The person sitting next to the emergency door was Albert Johnson. He was on his first plane trip. Just seeing his expression was something. Here is this inner-city kid on his first plane trip and the emergency door cracks open. He thought for sure we were all going to die. Everybody on the plane got sick. It is pretty hard with six guys in the bathroom throwing up. We finally landed, they fixed the problem and we went on to play Denver. We won too." — *Warren Rustand, 1963-65*.

Warren Rustand

DEAD SPOTS "Bear Down was always a great place for us. It was a noisy gym. There was a set of springs under the floor that helped make it easier to jump. But there were also dead spots. The opposing teams didn't know where the dead spots were. We tried to channel guards to the dead spots. They would be bouncing the ball and then it wouldn't come up very high. All of a sudden the ball wasn't there. That created turnover opportunities for us. We thought we were pretty clever."
— *Warren Rustand, 1963-65*.

GOING FOR A STROLL "(Arizona Coach Ben) Lindsey would always walk onto the court to get the referees' attention while the game was going on. In Tennessee, we

were just getting creamed, and Lindsey walks onto the court and steps in front of Frank Smith. By this time Frank is getting really frustrated and tells him, 'If you don't get off the court I will throw you off.'"
— *Brock Brunkhorst, 1981-85.*

WATCH YOUR STEP "When we went to Wyoming we played in their old gym. We called it the Cowchip Palace. The court was put right over a rodeo fairground. You walk out of the dressing room and you pretty much had to step off ding dong. If you lost the ball, it would go rolling over a tarp and into more dung. We would always get our manager to go get the balls for us. We weren't going to get into that stuff." — *Joe Nehls, 1978-80.*

WILDCAT QUIZ

20. Lute Olson's contract expires when?

ANYTHING FOR A BUCK "I would drive and earn extra money to go on road trips. You couldn't go any faster than 55 miles per hour. The group I was with were urging me to go faster and faster. There was a big line of cars, but I decided to pass them all up. As it turns out one of the cars was Coach Enke and I passed him up. I wasn't supposed to do that. The guys were giving me all kinds of fun about that. Coach Enke didn't like that."
— *Leo Johnson, 1949-51.*

THAT WAY "We were playing in the Cow Palace (in San Francisco). It was a big arena meant for basketball. I remember we were playing up and down when we got into this scramble. I was being knocked around trying to get to the ball. The referee called a foul and told me to go shoot the free throws. I head one way and the referee pointed me toward the other. I told him that is the wrong basket. I looked around for our bench and it was in the wrong place. I got all turned around. We were used to playing in little bitty places." — *Leo Johnson, 1949-51.*

CARS AND STRIKES "Tom (Tolbert) was on his way back home from Tucson over the summer, driving this old beat up old black sedan, a (Mercury) Cougar, I think. He was just outside of Blythe when it conked out, just died. It made the worst noise you would ever hear. (Craig) McMillan was following him. Tom pulled over way to the side of the road and into the desert and started putting all the stuff he could into Craig's car. He had to leave some of his stuff behind. When he was done Tom took out a baseball bat and started going to work on the car. He started hitting the car. He was so mad. He took off the license plate and just left it there. Before they took off, he left one of his hoop shoes and put it on the roof. A bunch of us would drive that same way because most of the team was from California. I came a day later. I did a double-take when I saw the car out in the desert. On the top of the car was a Nike shoe. I knew it was Tom's." — *Bruce Fraser on Tom Tolbert.*

WRITE YOUR NAME ON YOUR UNDERWEAR
"I was at McKale one day visiting with Lute. He was down changing and I walked with him back up to his office. He had changed back into his street clothes after practice. We were talking, going up the ramp when his underwear fell out from his bundle of clothes on the floor. I see them fall, but he didn't. I'm thinking, 'Do I want to pick up Lute Olson's underwear?' It was really the first time I saw him get red. I told him, 'You know, I could get a lot of money for these,' handed them to him, and he went back into his office." — *Dana Cooper, host of the "Lute Olson Show" since 1986.*

A LOOK BACK
"A few years ago we were doing personal stories on Lute and the assistants. We were doing two- to three-minute features on the coaches with their families. We went to their houses to shoot some footage of them playing with their kids and that kind of stuff. We sat down at Lute's house with his daughter, Steve, and Greg. Vicky was relating some rather tender stories, not about Lute Olson, but about her dad. Also in this feature we had Lute and Bobbi reminiscing about them as a young couple, what it was like struggling when they first got married. They talked about a big night out being going for pizza, but having to order water for the drinks because they couldn't afford sodas. When the feature was being aired I looked over at Lute and he had a bug in his eye. He kept scratching his eyes, you could tell he was misting up. You could tell looking back really meant something to him." — *Dana Cooper, host of the "Lute Olson Show" since 1986.*

A GOOD TEACHER
"He got me into this profession. I was teaching school in Chicago when he hired me as a graduate assistant. I thought maybe it would be a one or two year deal with him. He is my mentor. That's what he has been to me." — *Arizona assistant coach Jim Rosborough, who was an assistant with Olson in Iowa as well.*

Jim Rosborough

FISH BOWL
"It was a real challenge for him living in the fishbowl here. Just going out to dinner was tough for Lute." — *John Streif, Olson's trainer at Iowa.*

THE FIRST TIME ALWAYS MEANS MORE
"That first time does mean something special to me. It was a new system. Everyone coming in had to meld into a team situation. It wasn't a case of these guys having played together

before and now you have a new staff. In this situation, they didn't know the staff or their teammates. They were a very coachable group and very hungry. They were trying anything to get this program out of the 10 spot in the league.

"It was a team that I really felt strongly about because of the things they had to overcome. We were probably the best team in the conference by the end of the season. Oregon State won the league, but we beat them in double figures here in the second half and gave them all they wanted up there." — *Lute Olson on his 1983-84 team.*

SAY WHAT? "Joe Turner always hacked up the language. There was one time he was talking to one of his friends after we lost to Athletes in Action and he said, 'But that doesn't matter because it's an expedition game.' Then another time we are in Alaska and the waitress says, 'Do

McClutch always remembers Joe Turner smiling, or making others laugh.

you want soup or salad?' And Joe says, 'That sounds great.' Then there was somebody hiding behind an elevator to scare Joe. He didn't jump at all. Joe says, 'I knew you were there.' He was asked how he knew. Joe says, 'Because I have ESPN.'" — *Craig McMillan, 1985-88.*

SAY CHEESE "We were on a German riverboat, Coach Olson had his shirt off, and nobody could believe he had his shirt off to get some sun. We were all saying, 'We've got to get his picture.' Nobody had the guts to take his picture. (Ron) Curry finally said, 'I'll take his picture.' I think he figured he was leaving anyway (Curry transferred following the trip). As soon as Coach Olson saw Ron with the camera he reached back around to grab a shirt, but Ron caught him before he could say 'smile.'" — *source—to remain anonymous.*

SNOWED IN "We were up in Pullman when the game at Friel was called off because of the snow. It had blackened out the gym. We had to go to Bohler Gym (the equivalent to Bear Down). The game was set up in a matter of minutes. It was a broadcasting nightmare. They were already planning to have a large crowd. They couldn't get everybody in as 6,000 fans were there. Washington State had a pretty good team (in 1987). Craig McMillan came out and made his first six shots. The game was over by halftime. Bohler Gym was not prepared to handle a broadcast. We had to crawl under the bleachers to get to a phone line in a football assistant coach's office. We had to take the phone line up and around these poles and broadcast from a booth suspended from the rafters. It was a nightmare. We got it on the air." — *Brian Jefferies, KNST's Voice of the Wildcats since 1984.*

GOING UP—HOPEFULLY "At the NCAA tournament (in 1996) we were in Phoenix and Lute normally doesn't like to take advantage of game-day shoot-around at the gyms. The NCAA gives you only a half an hour and it's not worth driving to the gym, shooting for a half hour, and driving back. So he usually doesn't take advantage of the gym. Well, somebody was looking out the window and saw a basket and a court on the roof of a parking garage. Word got to Lute and he said that was perfect, we will go there and warm up. Not all the players could get into the elevator at once. Some had to wait. Well, the elevator got stuck in this five-story parking garage on a weekend before the game. There was nobody around. Olson had to pry the doors open to get the guys out." — *Brian Jefferies, KNST's Voice of the Wildcats since 1984.*

ORANGE DRILLS "We couldn't get into a gym one night to practice, so Coach Enke got out an orange to use for a basketball. The team assembled in the mezzanine of our hotel and ran through drills using the orange. It was, well, different." — *William Smitheran, 1953-54, told to the Arizona Daily Star.*

JERKS "Jerks draw jerks. Great kids draw great kids." — *Lute Olson*

WIMPY "He's not exactly the wimp on the beach waiting for you to kick sand in his face. He's not afraid to be physical." — *Lute Olson on Tom Tolbert.*

THE OLSON MODEL "As he stands by his bench — his body erect, his gaze ice — Lute Olson looks like the embodiment of a Delorean, right down to the gleaming silver top." — *San Francisco Chronicle.*

STAY OR ELSE "Leon Blevins played for a junior college for two years before coming here. Everybody wanted him, especially Arizona and Arizona State. He came to Arizona during rush week and Sigma Chi took him in. Leon wasn't really happy, though. He wanted to go back to Phoenix and play for Arizona State. The story I was told was that the Sigma Chi stole his clothes, and all his belongings and hid them and told him he wasn't going anywhere. They kept his stuff until he enrolled in school and signed up to play here." — *Leo Johnson, 1949-51.*

WHAT THEY SAY ABOUT LUTE
■ "I wouldn't have had a chance at a pro career without the experience I gained at Arizona under Lute Olson. I was about the last guy recruited in America in 1983, but there was something he liked, I guess. I improved each year and we progressed from nowhere to the Final Four. I look back and I know that being at Arizona was the best time of my life." — *Steve Kerr*
■ "I think the work ethic is the biggest thing he instilled in me. Even when you played a great game he was never satisfied. He was always making you work harder the next day. You could come off the court and be full of yourself, but that wasn't good enough for him. That has made me work harder. Look, it's paid off." — *Sean Elliott*
■ "He was a big factor in coming here. My high school coach thought highly of him. He brought Sean Elliott and those guys. They started to build a great program. I wanted to be a part of a winning program and he developed that here." — *Reggie Geary*
■ "I watch a lot of basketball and you look at a lot of stats of the all-time coaches and you see Dean Smith and

Jerry Tarkanian, coaches like that. For Coach Olson to get his 500th win that is a credit to him and for the things he has accomplished not only here, but at Iowa and Long Beach State. He works hard at what he does. I think it says something for him to have over 500 wins." — *Corey Williams.*

GET A HAIRCUT "I sat down in Coach Olson's office. It was the first time I was going to meet him. He walks in and I don't know whether I should stand up. He reaches out his hand to shake mine and he yanks me up right in front of him. He is a big guy. It was a little scary. I was a little intimidated. Lute is an impressive figure. He makes an impression when he walks into a room. I knew next time to stand up to shake his hand. He also said something about my hair, which was longer then. He said something like tomorrow you will come back with a haircut. It was like, 'Don't come back until you get a haircut.'" — *Brock Brunkhorst, 1981-85.*

DUCK! "In the Enke days I remember there was this player, Johnny Black. He had a few words with a Texas-El Paso guy. I think it was in 1940-41. After the game he went out of the locker room and slapped the guy, knocking him on his butt." — *Bob Felix, a follower of the Arizona basketball program since 1932 and a member of the Board of Directors of the Rebounders Club.*

HAVE SOME FUN "I can't say enough about Steve Kerr, Sean Elliott and Jud Buechler, guys like that. There is no question of the caliber of players they are. I would be a medium tall manager nowadays. But when we were players we were involved in a lot of school activities, the Bob Cats, student council, other student activity boards. These guys now are concentrating so hard on their sport and trying to get a degree that it is more of a profession. They miss out on their college days. It is college basketball or nothing." — *Bill Kemmeries, 1951-53.*

I BET YOU "It was a dumped game. They made it too close and we ended up winning. We got lucky. They could have killed us. They had just won the NCAA and NIT championships. We came out after winning that game and made speeches. Fred said it was the greatest win in Arizona history. We were told it was going to be scratched off our record." — *Bill Kemmeries on Arizona's historic 41-38 victory over CCNY.*

BEAT OF A DIFFERENT DRUM "On a road trip back in the Snowden days I purchased a drum. We didn't have any cheerleaders or band members on the road with us. I

purchased the drum. That night we painted the Wildcat on it. We would beat it at all the games. I did that for five and a half years. Finally the WAC board went as far as to declare that fans could not carry personal instruments into the arenas. By that time I was glad they did."
— *George Kalil, long time Arizona fan, booster and 24-year travel companion.*

MONEY IN THE BANK "The individual player of one game that I remember was Eric Money against El Paso. Prior to the game *Sports Illustrated* had asked Eric about UTEP. Eric said he didn't like the way they played. They played a really slow-paced game. Eric was a big city guy (who liked to run). Fans from UTEP took that *Sports Illustrated* article and copied it into a 100 different copies and put it up everywhere, on poles, buildings, everywhere you look with Eric saying he didn't like UTEP. When we got to the game they booed Eric. He got mad. He trounced them. He took over. It was the most unbelievable sight I ever have seen. The more they yelled at him the better he played. He didn't pass the ball to anybody. He would get the ball and shoot. That got the UTEP fans even madder." — *George Kalil.*

GOOD CREDENTIALS "In (Ben) Lindsey's case things just got so out of hand there never was a chance. He came from a good background, with good references. (Phoenix Suns General Manager) Jerry Colangelo was one of his references. Lindsey had other influential friends in the state. (Former Senator) Dennis Deconcini wrote him a letter of recommendation. The circumstances here never would be easy for him, or anybody." — *George Kalil.*

ROAD TRIP MISHAPS
■ "In Hawaii we had an extra day so we looked around the island. Eric Money was on the bus asleep. I woke him up and said, 'You are missing all of this.' He started going back to sleep and said, 'I saw it yesterday.' He had slipped out of the hotel the day before and saw the sights by himself."
■ "In Laramie during the game the fans were getting at a feverish pitch. I saw three cans of filled beers, thrown from the stands, hit the court. You know fans are too drunk when they start throwing cans of full beer."
■ "Some fans in the WAC would put matches on copper pennies and throw them at you. It would leave a mark on your skin if they hit you."
■ "At 2 o'clock in the morning we were in our bus when the police pulled us over. There were sirens all over the place. It was scary. They thought we were a bunch of strike breakers going to a coal mine." — *Accounts from George Kalil.*

BACK HOME "The Final Four was great for me. I was going back home to Kansas City. That was pretty exciting. Here I was just out of high school and now I'm at the Final Four. I was in another world. It was so exciting for me because there was no pressure. I knew I wasn't going to play. I got to really enjoy everything about the Final Four. I had my eyes open for all the events. I let my mind wander, something the guys who were starting couldn't." — *Matt Muehlebach, 1988-91.*

Matt Muehlebach seldom gave up.

HIGH EXPECTATIONS-LOW RESULTS "The fans did expect a lot. The rest of the players felt that way too. That is not to say we didn't have good years, but we were all disappointed we never won the championship or made it back to the Final Four. We were more disappointed than the fans. We didn't meet our goals. We had the talent and the desire to do it. The 1989 season was the biggest disappointment. The team still had some of the players from the previous year. I'm not going to say we were better, but I think we had the ingredients we needed to be as good as that team. When we lost (to UNLV) that really hurt." — *Matt Muehlebach, 1988-91.*

By the Numbers

The statistics found here are provided by the University of Arizona Sports Information department and are updated through the 1995-96 school year.

SEASON BY SEASON SUMMARY

Year	Coach	W	L	Captains
1904-05	Orin Kates	1	0	Charles O. Brown, Jr.
1905-06	Orin KatesIntra-Squad Games only			Charles O. Brown, Jr.
1906-07	Unknown	3	1	Hugo E. Birkner
1907-08	Unknown	1	2	Jose Salazar
1908-09	Unknown	1	1	George Roberson
1909-10	Unknown	2	2	Ernest O. Blades
1910-11	Unknown	3	0	George Spaulding
1911-12	Frank L. Kleenberger	2	2	James Sullivan
1912-13	Raymond L. Quigley	3	2	Normal G. Hayhurst
1913-14	Raymond L. Quigley	7	2	Ralph L. Reynolds
1914-15	J.F. McKale	9	0	Leo F. Cloud
1915-16	J.F. McKale	5	0	Alma P. Sessions
1916-17	J.F. McKale	10	2	James S. Maffeo
1917-18	J.F. McKale	3	2	Albin A. Iselin
1918-19	J.F. McKale	6	3	J. Prugh Herndon
1919-20	J.F. McKale	9	5	A. Louis Slonaker
1920-21	J.F. McKale	7	0	Thomas J. Wallace
1921-22	James H. Pierce	10	2	Bret H. Locking
1922-23	James H. Pierce	17	3	Harold C. Tovrea
1923-24	Basil Stanley	14	3	Harold C. Tovrea
1924-25	Walter Davis	7	4	Marvin C. Clark
1925-26	Fred A. Enke	6	7	Frank Brookshier
1926-27	Fred A. Enke	13	4	Frank Brookshier
1927-28	Fred A. Enke	13	3	George Sorenson
1928-29	Fred A. Enke	19	4	George Sorenson
1929-30	Fred A. Enke	15	6	Waldo Dicus/Neil Goodman
1930-31	Fred A. Enke	9	6	Myron Nelson/George Ridgway
1931-32	Fred A. Enke	18	2	Jack Raffety

Border Conference

Year	Coach	W	L	Conf. W	Conf. L	Place	Captains
1932-33	Fred A. Enke	19	5	7	3	1st	Edgar Crismon
1933-34	Fred A. Enke	18	9	9	3	2nd	George Johnson
1934-35	Fred A. Enke	11	8	5	7	4th	Walter Scholtzhauer
1935-36	Fred A. Enke	16	7	11	5	1st	Elmer Vickers
1936-37	Fred A. Enke	14	11	9	7	3rd	Ralph Warford
1937-38	Fred A. Enke	13	8	9	7	2nd	Walter Heim/Lorry DeGrazia
1938-39	Fred A. Enke	12	11	8	10	5th	Dan Clarke
1939-40	Fred A. Enke	15	10	12	4	1st	Carl Berra/George Jordan
1940-41	Fred A. Enke	11	7	9	6	2nd	Wilmer Harper
1941-42	Fred A. Enke	9	13	6	10	6th	Bob Ruman/Vince Cullen
1942-43	Fred A. Enke	22	2	16	2	T1st	George Genung
1943-44	Fred A. Enke	12	2	Not held			George Genung
1944-45	Fred A. Enke	7	11	Not held			Harold Goodman
1945-46	Fred A. Enke	25	5	14	3	1st	Marvin Borodkin
1946-47	Fred A. Enke	18	3	14	2	1st	Linc Richmond/Morris Udall
1947-48	Fred A. Enke	17	10	12	4	1st	Fred W. Enke/John Padelford
1948-49	Fred A. Enke	17	11	13	3	1st	Hillard Crum/William Mann
1949-50	Fred A. Enke	24	5	14	2	1st	Leon Blevins
1950-51	Fred A. Enke	22	6	15	1	1st	Leo Johnson/Bob Honea
1951-52	Fred A. Enke	8	16	6	8	T3rd	Roger Johnson
1952-53	Fred A. Enke	13	11	11	3	T1st	Bill Kemmeries
1953-54	Fred A. Enke	14	10	8	4	3rd	John Bruner
1954-55	Fred A. Enke	8	17	3	9	6th	George Rountree/Eli Lazovich/Jim Brower
1955-56	Fred A. Enke	11	15	6	6	5th	Bill Wagner/Bill Reeves
1956-57	Fred A. Enke	13	13	.5	5	3rd	Bill Reeves
1957-58	Fred A. Enke	10	15	4	6	T4th	Ed Nymeyer
1958-59	Fred A. Enke	4	22	1	9	6th	Dick Mower/Louis Hopkins
1959-60	Fred A. Enke	10	14	4	6	4th	Jon Conner/Ernie McCray
1960-61	Fred A. Enke	11	15	5	5	3rd	Marv Dutt/Bill Weese

Western Athletic Conference

Year	Coach	W	L	Conf.	Place	Captains
1961-62	Bruce Larson	12	14	No games		Joe Skaisgir
1962-63	Bruce Larson	13	13	3	7 T5th	Wes Flynn
1963-64	Bruce Larson	15	11	4	6 4th	Warren Rustand
1964-65	Bruce Larson	17	9	5	5 T2nd	Warren Rustand
1965-66	Bruce Larson	15	11	5	5 3rd	Harvey Fox/Bob Hansen/Bob Spahn
1966-67	Bruce Larson	8	17	3	7 5th	Mike Abound
1967-68	Bruce Larson	11	13	4	6 T4th	Mike Kordick/Bill Davis
1968-69	Bruce Larson	17	10	5	5 3rd	Jim Hansen
1969-70	Bruce Larson	12	14	8	6 4th	Mickey Foster
1970-71	Bruce Larson	10	16	3	11 8th	Tom Lee
1971-72	Bruce Larson	6	20	4	10 7th	Bruce Anderson/Jim Huckestein
1972-73	Fred Snowden	16	10	9	5 T2nd	Lynard Harris/Tom Lawson
1973-74	Fred Snowden	19	7	9	5 T2nd	Ron Allen/Eric Money/Coniel Norman
1974-75	Fred Snowden	22	7	9	5 3rd	Dave Burns/Steve Kanner
1975-76	Fred Snowden	24	9	11	3 1st	Al Fleming/Jim Rappis
1976-77	Fred Snowden	21	6	10	4 2nd	Bob Elliott/Len Gordy/Herman Harris
1977-78	Fred Snowden	15	11	6	8 T4th	Phil Taylor

Pacific-10 Conference

Year	Coach	W	L	Conf.	Place	Captains
1978-79	Fred Snowden	16	11	10	8 T4th	Larry Demic
1979-80	Fred Snowden	12	15	6	12 6th	Joe Nehls
1980-81	Fred Snowden	13	14	8	10 T5th	Russell Brown
1981-82	Fred Snowden	9	18	4	14 T8th	Frank Smith
1982-83	Ben Lindsey	4	24	1	17 10th	John Belobraydic
1983-84	Lute Olson	11	17	8	10 8th	Pete Williams/Eddie Smith
1984-85	Lute Olson	21	10	12	6 T3rd	Brock Brunkhorst
1985-86	Lute Olson	23	9	14	4 1st	Steve Kerr/John Edgar
1986-87	Lute Olson	18	12	13	5 2nd	Bruce Fraser
1987-88	Lute Olson	35	3	17	1 1st	Steve Kerr
1988-89	Lute Olson	29	4	17	1 1st	Sean Elliott/Anthony Cook
1989-90	Lute Olson	25	7	15	3 T1st	Jud Buechler
1990-91	Lute Olson	28	7	14	4 1st	Matt Muehlebach
1991-92	Lute Olson	24	7	13	5 3rd	Sean Rooks/Wayne Womack/Matt Othick
1992-93	Lute Olson	24	4	17	1 1st	Chris Mills
1993-94	Lute Olson	29	6	14	4 1st	Kevin Flanagan/Khalid Reeves/Damon Stoudamire
1994-95	Lute Olson	23	8	13	5 2nd	Reggie Geary/Ray Owes/Damon Stoudamire
1995-96	Lute Olson	26	7	13	5 2nd	Reggie Geary/Corey Williams/Ben Davis/Joe McLean

COACHES' ALL-TIME RECORD

Years	Coach	Collegiate			Non-Collegiate			Overall		
		W	L	Pct.	W	L	Pct.	W	L	Pct.
2	Orin A. Kates	0	0	.000	1	0+	1.000	1	0	1.000
5	Unknown	0	0	.000	10	6	.625	10	6	.625
1	Frank Kleeberger	0	0	.000	2	2	.500	2	2	.500
2	Raymond L. Quigley	2	0	1.000	8	4	.667	10	4	.714
7	J.F. McKale	13	5	.722	36	7	.837	49	12	.803
2	James H. Pierce	18	4	.818	9	1	.900	27	5	.844
1	Basil Stanley	11	3	.786	3	0	1.000	14	3	.824
1	Walter Davis	4	3	.571	3	1	.750	7	4	.636
36	Fred Enke	402	300	.573	109	18	.858	511	318	.616
11	Bruce Larson	136	148	.479	1	1	.500	137	148	.481
10	Fred Snowden	167	108	.607	6	2	.750	173	110	.611
1	Ben Lindsey	4	24	.143	0	1	.000	4	25	.138
13	Lute Olson	316	101	.757	49	16	.753	363	117	.756
91	Collective Group	1,073	696	.606	237	59	.800	1,310	755	.634

ARIZONA NCAA SCORES

Year	Opponent	Result	Score	Year	Opponent	Result	Score
1951	Kansas State	L	61-59	1988	Cornell	W	90-60
1976	Georgetown	W	83-76	1988	Seton Hall	W	84-55
1976	UNLV	W	114-109	1988	Iowa	W	99-79
1976	UCLA	L	82-66	1988	North Carolina	W	70-52
1977	Southern Illinois	L	81-77	1988	Oklahoma	L	86-78
1985	Alabama	L	50-41	1989	Robert Morris	W	94-60
1986	Auburn	L	73-63	1989	Clemson	W	94-68
1987	UTEP	L	98-91	1989	UNLV	L	68-67

Year	Opponent	Result	Score
1990	South Florida	W	79-67
1990	Alabama	L	77-55
1991	St. Francis	W	93-80
1991	BYU	W	76-61
1991	Seton Hall	L	81-77
1992	East Tennessee State	L	87-80
1993	Santa Clara	L	64-61
1994	Loyola (Md.)	W	81-55
1994	Virginia	W	71-58

Year	Opponent	Result	Score
1994	Louisville	W	82-70
1994	Missouri	W	92-72
1994	Arkansas	L	91-82
1995	Miami (Ohio)	L	71-62
1996	Valparaiso	W	90-51
1996	Iowa	W	87-73
1996	Kansas	L	83-80
15 years	32 Opponents		17-15

TEAM RECORDS

MOST POINTS SCORED

Game — 133 vs Duquesne, 1987-88 (133-78)
Half — 69 at Utah, 1973-74 (second)
Season — 3,234, 1987-88 (38 games)
Season margin for — 22.9, 1987-88 (85.1 to 62.2)
Season margin against — 15.7, 1958-59 (63.2 to 78.9)
Avg. pts per game — 89.3, 1993-94 (3,124 in 35 games)

LARGEST VICTORY MARGIN

Game — 60, Adams State, 1976-77 (115-55)

LARGEST MARGIN OF DEFEAT

Game — 74, at Utah, 1955-56 (45-119)

FIELD GOALS

Game — 54 vs Duquesne, 1987-88 (att. 86)
Half — 30 vs Adams State, 1976-77 (att 53, first)
Season — 1,147, 1987-88 (38 games)
Per game — 36.4, 1973-74 (946 in 26 games)

FIELD GOALS ATTEMPTED

Game — 110, vs Northern Arizona, 1963-64 (made 43)
Half — 5,7 vs Northern Arizona, 1963-64 (made 24, second)
Season — 2,238, 1975-76 (33 games)
Per game — 67.8, 1975-76 (33 games)

FIELD GOAL PERCENTAGE

Game — .714, vs Oregon State, 1983-84 (25-of-35)
Half — .800, at California, 1989-90 (20-of-25, first)
Season high — .545, 1987-88 (1,147-2,106)
Season low — .317, 1954-55 (597-1,880)

3-POINT FIELD GOALS

Game — 15, at Oregon, 1991-92 (att. 24)
Half — 10, at Oregon, 1991-92 (att 14, first)
Season — 279, 1993-94 (35 games)
Per game — 8, 1993-94 (279 in 35 games)

3-POINT FIELD GOALS ATTEMPTED

Game — 32, vs Arkansas, 1993-94 (made 6)
Half — 19, vs Oregon, 1986-87 (made 3, second)
Season — 787, 1993-94, (35 games)
Per game — 22.5, 1993-94 (787 in 35 games)

3-POINT FIELD GOALS PERCENTAGE

Game — .857, vs Arkansas-Little Rock, 1986-87 (6-of-7)
Half — 1.000, at Washington State, 1987-88 (5-of-5)
Season high — .483, 1987-88 (254-526)
Season low — .355, 1993-94 (279-787)

FREE THROWS

Game — 41, vs Arizona State, 1955-56 (att. 51)
Season — 686, 1987-88 (att 932 in 38 games)
Per game — 21.7, 1952-53 (made 585 in 27 games)

FREE THROWS ATTEMPTED

Game — 52, vs Memphis State, 1964-65 (Made 35)
Season — 967, 1990-91 (35 games)
Per game — 34.7, 1952-53 (938 in 27 games)

FREE THROWS PERCENTAGE

Game — 1.000, vs USC, 1972-73 (13-of-13)
(Min 20): .963, vs San Diego Navy, 1951-52 (26-of-27)
(Min 30): .868, vs BYU, 1962-63 (33-of-38)
Season high — .741, 1988-89 (627-846)
Season low — .578, 1945-46 (279-485)

REBOUNDS

Game — 102, at Northern Arizona, 1950-51
Margin for — 84, at Northern Arizona, 1950-51 (102-18)
Margin against — 42, at New Mexico, 1964-65 (24-68)
Season — 1,786, 1950-51 (30 games)
Per game — 59.5, 1950-51 (1,788 in 30 games)
Season margin for — 19.3, 1950-51, (59.5-40.2)
Season margin against — 7.2, 1960-61 (50.8-58)

PERSONAL FOULS

Game — 50, at Northern Arizona, 1952-53
Fewest — 6, at Bradley, 1963-64
Disqualified — 7, at West Texas State, 1951-52
Most fouls season — 720, 1950-51, (30 games)
Most Per game — 24.0, 1950-51 (720 in 30 games)
Fewest fouls season — 461, 1967-68 (24 games)
Fewest fouls game — 14.9, 1985-86 (478 in 32 games)

TURNOVERS

Fewest — 4, vs Washington State, 1991-92; at UCLA, 1985-86; vs UCLA, 1989-90
Most — 37, at New Mexico, 1978-79
Season high — 563, 1974-75 (26 games); 1975-76 (33 games)
Arizona season high per game — 21.6, 1974-75 (563 in 26 games)
Season low — 331, 1979-80 (27 games)
Arizona season low per game — 10.5, 1985-86 (337 in 32 games)

OVERTIMES

Most — 3, vs Utah, 1972-73 (101-95); vs Colorado, 1965-66 (73-79); vs Bradley, 1964-65 (85-83)
Points — 20 vs Stanford, 1979-80

SERIES RECORD

Opponent	W	L	First Game	Last Game	Opponent	W	L	First Game	Last Game
Adams State	1	0	1977	1977	Jacksonville	0	1	1970	1970
Air Force	2	4	1959	1968	Kansas	0	3	1980	1996
Alabama	0	2	1985	1990	Kansas State	3	8	1951	1982
Alaska-Anchorage	1	0	1995	1995	Kentucky	0	2	1946	1994
Arizona State	116	72	1914	1996	Lamar	1	1	1980	1981
Arkansas	2	6	1949	1995	LaSalle	1	2	1950	1995
Arkansas-Little Rock	1	0	1988	1988	LaVerne	2	0	1932	1933
Auburn	0	1	1986	1986	Long Beach State	3	0	1988	1995
Austin Peay	1	0	1991	1991	Long Island	1	0	1951	1951
Baylor	4	3	1948	1994	Louisiana State	1	1	1991	1992
Beloit	1	1	1950	1954	Louisville	1	2	1949	1994
Boston College	2	0	1986	1994	Loyola (Ill.)	1	0	1989	1989
Bowling Green	0	1	1956	1956	Loyola (Md.)	1	0	1994	1994
Bradley	3	7	1948	1965	Loyola-Marymount	7	4	1937	1985
Brigham Young	18	17	1952	1991	Marquette	1	1	1974	1994
Butler	1	0	1971	1971	Maryland	1	0	1964	1964
Cal-Poly Pomona	2	0	1966	1974	Memphis State	2	3	1953	1966
CS-Bakersfield	1	0	1973	1973	Miami (Fla.)	2	0	1986	1990
CS-Fullerton	2	1	1976	1984	Miami (Ohio)	0	2	1947	1995
CS-Hayward	2	0	1965	1981	Michigan	5	1	1958	1995
CS-Los Angeles	4	5	1958	1972	Michigan State	2	1	1958	1990
Canisius	1	3	1948	1954	Midwestern	2	0	1976	1980
Centenary	2	1	1953	1974	Minnesota	0	4	1952	1995
Charleston	1	0	1981	1981	Mississippi	0	1	1953	1953
Cincinnati	3	0	1976	1996	Mississippi State	1	0	1971	1971
Clemson	1	0	1989	1989	Missouri	1	1	1985	1994
Colorado	4	8	1961	1975	Montana	1	0	1995	1995
Colorado State	14	11	1955	1978	Montana State	1	1	1940	1982
Columbia	1	0	1975	1975	Morehead State	1	0	1947	1947
Cornell	1	0	1988	1988	Murray State	1	1	1956	1957
Creighton	1	1	1968	1969	Nebraska	1	2	1961	1970
Dayton	1	1	1951	1992	UNLV	4	9	1973	1990
Delaware	1	0	1993	1993	New Mexico	82	39	1917	1993
Denver	3	1	1962	1986	New Mexico State	54	38	1917	1972
DePaul	0	2	1930	1934	New Mexico Tech	10	0	1920	1942
DePauw	1	0	1971	1971	New Orleans	3	0	1992	1994
Detroit	1	1	1976	1977	New York	0	1	1952	1952
Drake	1	1	1934	1975	Niagara	0	1	1954	1954
Duke	3	2	1962	1991	North Carolina	1	2	1949	1989
Duquesne	1	3	1948	1988	North Texas State	1	0	1968	1970
East Carolina	1	0	1975	1975	Northern Arizona	84	27	1919	1992
E. Tennessee State	1	1	1991	1992	Northern Colorado	1	1	1960	1962
Eastern Michigan	2	0	1969	1978	Northern Illinois	2	0	1973	1975
Eastern New Mexico	1	0	1961	1961	Northwestern	2	0	1977	1979
Evansville	3	1	1964	1992	Notre Dame	2	1	1934	1994
Florida State	1	2	1970	1995	Occidental	5	1	1931	1935
Fordham	1	1	1970	1994	Ohio	0	1	1956	1956
Fort Hays State	1	0	1984	1984	Ohio State	0	1	1972	1972
Fresno State	2	3	1960	1981	Oklahoma	1	2	1988	1990
Georgetown	2	1	1976	1995	Oklahoma City	1	1	1934	1957
Georgia Tech	0	1	1991	1991	Oklahoma State	2	0	1994	1995
Grand Canyon	4	0	1978	1981	Old Dominion	1	0	1976	1976
Hamline	3	0	1956	1963	Pacific	3	1	1958	1977
Hardin-Simmons	24	14	1940	1967	Pan American	1	1	1984	1985
Harvard	2	0	1967	1978	Penn State	1	0	1990	1990
Hawaii	2	0	1976	1992	Pepperdine	4	0	1965	1991
Hawaii-Hilo	2	0	1985	1986	Pittsburgh	3	2	1949	1992
Hawaii-Pacific	2	0	1985	1986	Pomona	2	0	1932	1933
Houston	3	4	1968	1995	Portland State	1	0	1976	1976
Houston-Baptist	1	0	1985	1985	Princeton	1	0	1986	1986
Idaho	4	0	1974	1979	Providence	2	2	1982	1993
Idaho State	3	4	1959	1980	Purdue	4	4	1934	1990
Illinois	3	4	1967	1988	Regis	1	1	1960	1961
Illinois-Wesleyan	1	1	1982	1983	Richmond	1	0	1995	1995
Iowa	3	5	1958	1996	Rhode Island	2	0	1993	1995
Iowa State	2	3	1970	1991	Robert Morris	1	0	1995	1995

Opponent	W	L	First Game	Last Game
Rutgers	2	0	1992	1995
St. Bonaventure	1	0	1987	1987
St. Francis (Pa.)	1	1	1968	1991
St. Francis (NY)	0	1	1948	1948
St. Joseph's (Pa.)	2	0	1948	1994
St. Louis	0	1	1934	1934
St. Mary's (Calif.)	1	2	1949	1952
San Diego	1	0	1973	1973
San Diego State	15	5	1946	1987
San Francisco	1	4	1949	1973
San Francisco State	1	0	1985	1985
San Jose State	10	4	1937	1985
Santa Clara	4	3	1937	1994
Seattle	5	2	1963	1971
Seton Hall	1	1	1988	1991
South Florida	1	0	1990	1990
Southeast Oklahoma	0	1	1940	1940
Southern Alabama	0	1	1972	1972
Southern Illinois	2	1	1966	1977
Southern Methodist	3	0	1974	1977
Southern Mississippi	2	0	1951	1955
Southwestern	0	1	1934	1934
Southwestern Louisiana	1	0	1979	1979
Syracuse	1	2	1988	1995
Temple	2	0	1989	1992
Tennessee	0	3	1957	1984
Texas	0	2	1950	1972
UTEP	58	30	1920	1995
Texas-San Antonio	1	1	1983	1986
Texas A&M	5	0	1950	1995
Texas Christian	0	2	1940	1953
Texas Tech	22	28	1934	1995
Towson State	1	0	1995	1995
Tulane	1	0	1939	1939
Tulsa	1	2	1955	1986

Opponent	W	L	First Game	Last Game
UC-Davis	1	0	1975	1975
UC-Riverside	2	0	1972	1981
UC-Santa Barbara	6	3	1956	1981
U.S. International	1	0	1982	1982
Utah	17	27	1954	1994
Utah State	0	3	1959	1964
Valparaiso	1	0	1996	1996
Vanderbilt	0	1	1957	1957
Villanova	2	1	1968	1991
Virginia	1	0	1994	1994
Wayne State	1	0	1947	1947
Weber State	3	0	1967	1970
West Texas State	20	16	1940	1962
West Virginia	3	1	1949	1993
Western Illinois	1	0	1991	1991
Western New Mexico	3	3	1941	1962
Whittier	11	1	1924	1951
Wichita	1	0	1952	1952
Wichita State	0	1	1955	1955
Wisconsin	1	1	1963	1967
Wyoming	17	15	1963	1978

ARIZONA VS PAC-10

Opponent	W	L	First Game	Last Game
Arizona State	116	72	1914	1996
California	28	21	1924	1996
Oregon	24	13	1979	1996
Oregon State	27	13	1976	1996
Stanford	33	34	1938	1996
UCLA	18	32	1923	1996
USC	37	28	1922	1996
Washington	24	13	1965	1996
Washington State	29	10	1960	1996

INDIVIDUAL RECORDS

POINTS

Game — 46, Ernie McCray vs Cal State-LA, 2-6-60
Season — 848, Khalid Reeves, 1994 (35 games)
Career — 2,555, Sean Elliott, 1986-89 (133 games)

POINTS PER GAME

Season — 24.2, Khalid Reeves, 1994 (848 in 35 games)
Career — 23.9, Coniel Norman, 1972-74 (1,194 in 50 games)

FIELD GOALS

Game — 19, Coniel Norman at BYU, 1-25-74 (att. 31)
Season — 276, Khalid Reeves, 1994
Career — 896, Sean Elliott 1986-89

FIELD GOALS ATTEMPTED

Game — 32, Bill Kemmeries at Hardin-Simmons, 2-16-52 (Made 14)
Season — 572, Khalid Reeves, 1994
Career — 1,750, Sean Elliott, 1986-89

FIELD GOAL PERCENTAGE

Minimum of 10 attempts
Game — 1.000, Al Fleming vs Midwestern, 12-1-75 (10-for-10)
More than 10 attempts
Game — .933, Brian Williams at UCLA 2-10-91, (14-for-15)
Season — .667, Al Fleming, 1974 (136-204)

Career — .605, Pete Williams, 1983-85 (296-489)

3-POINT FIELD GOALS

Game — 7, Damon Stoudamire at Stanford, 1-14-95; Matt Othick vs Temple, 2-23-92; Craig McMillan at Washington, 2-21-87
Season — 114, Steve Kerr, 1988
Career — 272, Damon Stoudamire, 1992-95

3-POINT FIELD GOALS ATTEMPTED

Game — 15, Damon Stoudamire vs California, 2-12-95
Season — 265, Damon Stoudamire, 1994
Career — 667, Damon Stoudamire, 1992-95

FREE THROWS

Game — 15, Sean Elliott vs Stanford, 3-12-88 (att 16)
Season — 211, Khalid Reeves, 1994 (att 264)
Career — 623, Sean Elliott, 1986-89 (att 786)

FREE THROWS ATTEMPTED

Game — 20, Bob Elliott vs Arizona State, 2-2-74 (made 14)
Season — 264, Khalid Reeves, 1994 (made 211)
Career — 786, Sean Elliott, 1986-89 (made 623)

REBOUNDS

Game — 26, Bill Reeves vs UCSB, 2-1-56; Joe Skaisgir vs Cal. St.-LA, 1-31-62
Season — 373, Leo Johnson, 1951
Career — 1,190, Al Fleming, 1972-76

PERSONAL FOULS

Season — 113, Leo Johnson, 1950
Season per game — 4.3, Bill Reeves, 1957
Season times disqualified — 13, Bill Reeves, 1957
Career — 352, Al Fleming, 1972-76
Career/games — 3.9, Bill Reeves, 1954-57 (298 in 77 games)
Career times disqualified — 34, Junior Crum, 1942-44, 46-47 (101 games)

ASSISTS

Game — 19, Russell Brown vs Grand Canyon, 12-8-79
Season — 247, Russell Brown, 1979
Career — 810, Russell Brown, 1977-81

BLOCKED SHOTS

Game — 7, Anthony Cook vs UTEP, 3-13-87
Season — 84, Anthony Cook, 1989
Career — 278, Anthony Cook, 1986-89

STEALS

Game — 7, Russell Brown vs UC-Riverside, 12-12-80
7, Puntus Wilson vs Stanford, 3-3-83
7, Reggie Geary at Washington, 3-4-95
Season — 67, Ken Lofton, 1989, Reggie Geary, 1996
Career — 208, Reggie Geary, 1993-96

TOP 10s

SCORING, CAREER

Average	Player	Years
23.9	Coniel Norman	1973-74
19.9	Joe Skaisgir	1960-62
19.2	Sean Elliott	1986-89
18.7	Bob Elliott	1974-77
18.6	Eric Money	1973-74
17.8	Ernie McCray	1957-60
17.2	Chris Mills	1991-93
16.8	Joe Nehls	1977-80
16.4	Bill Davis	1966-68

FIELD GOALS, CAREER

No.	Player	Years
892	Sean Elliott	1986-89
808	Bob Elliott	1974-77
688	Al Fleming	1973-76
646	Khalid Reeves	1991-94
629	Anthony Cook	1986-89
614	Damon Stoudamire	1992-95
615	Chris Mills	1991-93
582	Bill Warner	1968-71
569	Joe Nehls	1977-80
553	Steve Kerr	1984-88

FREE THROWS, CAREER

No.	Player	Years
623	Sean Elliott	1986-89
515	Bob Elliott	1974-77
447	Khalid Reeves	1991-994
392	Sean Rooks	1988-92
389	Al Fleming	1973-76
351	Ed Nymeyer	1956-58
349	Damon Stoudamire	1992-95
332	Anthony Cook	1986-89
329	Ernie McCray	1957-60
298	Bill Warner	1969-71

FIELD GOAL PERCENTAGE, CAREER

Average	Player	Years
.605	Pete Williams	1984-85
.597	Joseph Blair	1993-95
.591	Brian Williams	1990-91
.582	Al Fleming	1973-76
.575	Anthony Cook	1986-89
.558	Sean Rooks	1988-92
.553	Larry Demic	1975-79
.551	Steve Kerr	1984-88
.547	Jud Buechler	1987-90
.538	Ben Davis	1995-96

FIELD GOAL PERCENTAGE, CAREER

No.	Player	Years
1,750	Sean Elliott	1986-89
1,512	Bob Elliott	1974-77
1,349	Khalid Reeves	1991-94
1,343	Damon Stoudamire	1992-95
1,263	Bill Warner	1968-71
1,250	Linc Richmond	1943-49
1,200	Joe Nehls	1977-80
1,194	Chris Mills	1991-93
1,181	Al Fleming	1973-76
1,175	Ernie McCray	1959-60

FREE THROWS, CAREER

No.	Player	Years
786	Sean Elliott	1986-89
767	Bob Elliott	1974-77
590	Sean Rooks	1988-92
586	Khalid Reeves	1991-94
537	Ernie McCray	1957-60
522	Al Fleming	1973-76
515	Anthony Cook	1986-89
495	Ed Nymeyer	1956-58
448	Frank Smith	1980-83
434	Damon Stoudamire	1992-95

FREE THROW PERCENTAGE, CAREER

Pct.	Player	Years
.872	Dylan Rigdon	1993-94
.854	Joe Nehls	1976-80
.820	Mickey Foster	1967-70
.815	Steve Kerr	1984-88
.810	Warren Rustand	1962-65
.805	Bob Spahn	1963-66
.804	Damon Stoudamire	1992-95
.792	Matt Muehlebach	1988-91
.793	Sean Elliott	1986-89
.787	Craig McMillan	1985-88

REBOUNDS, CAREER

No.	Player	Years
1,190	Al Fleming	1973-76
1,083	Bob Elliott	1974-77
861	Anthony Cook	1986-89
837	Bill Reeves	1954-57
824	Ernie McCray	1957-60
808	Sean Elliott	1986-89
755	Albert Johnson	1962-65
737	Tom Lee	1969-71
723	Frank Smith	1980-83
721	Ray Owes	1992-95

REBOUNDING AVG., CAREER

Average	Player	Years
11.2	Joe Skaisgir	1960-62
10.8	Ernie McCray	1957-60
10.7	Bill Reeves	1954-57
10.4	Al Fleming	1973-76
9.9	Albert Johnson	1962-65
9.5	Eddie Myers	1968-71
9.5	Bob Elliott	1973-77
9.2	Pete Williams	1983-85
9.1	Bill Davis	1966-68

3-POINT FIELD GOALS ATTEMPTED, CAREER

No.	Player	Years
677	Damon Stoudamire	1992-95
489	Khalid Reeves	1991-94
485	Matt Othick	1989-92
389	Matt Muehlebach	1988-91
327	Chris Mills	1991-93
327	Sean Elliott	1986-89
265	Craig McMillan	1985-88
235	Ken Lofton	1986-89
211	Chris Mills	1991-93
214	Reggie Geary	1993-96
199	Steve Kerr	1984-88

3-POINT FIELD GOAL PERCENTAGE, CAREER

Pct.	Player	Years	3FGM-A
.573	Steve Kerr	1984-88	114-199
.428	Sean Elliott	1986-89	140-237
.424	Harvey Mason	1987-90	50-118
.419	Matt Muehlebach	1988-91	199-251
.411	Craig McMillan	1985-88	109-265
.402	Damon Stoudamire	1992-95	272-677
.394	Matt Othick	1989-92	191-485
.385	Chris Mills	1991-93	126-327
.380	Khalid Reeves	1991-94	186-489

3-POINT FIELD GOALS MADE, CAREER

No.	Player	Years
272	Damon Stoudamire	1992-95
191	Matt Othick	1989-92
186	Khalid Reeves	1991-94
163	Matt Muehlebach	1988-91
140	Sean Elliott	1986-89
126	Chris Mills	1991-93
114	Steve Kerr	1984-88
109	Craig McMillan	1985-88
87	Ken Lofton	1986-89
67	Reggie Geary	1993-96

ASSISTS, CAREER

No.	Player	Years
810	Russell Brown	1978-81
663	Damon Stoudamire	1992-95
552	Matt Othick	1989-92
458	Matt Muehlebach	1988-91
451	Sean Elliott	1986-89
443	Steve Kerr	1984-88
414	Brock Brunkhorst	1982-85
396	Khalid Reeves	1991-94
329	Ken Lofton	1986-89
329	Reggie Geary	1993-96

SCORING AVERAGE, SEASON

Average	Player	Year
24.2	Khalid Reeves	1993-94
24.0	Coniel Norman	1972-73
23.9	Ernie McCray	1959-60
23.8	Coniel Norman	1973-74
23.3	Bob Elliott	1974-75
22.8	Damon Stoudamire	1994-95

Average	Player	Year
22.2	Sean Elliott	1988-89
20.9	Bob Warner	1970-71
20.4	Chris Mills	1992-93
20.3	Joe Skaisgir	1961-62
	Bill Warner	1969-70
20.0	Herman Harris	1976-77

FIELD GOALS MADE, SEASON

No.	Player	Year
276	Khalid Reeves	1993-94
273	Bob Elliott	1974-75
264	Coniel Norman	1973-74
263	Sean Elliott	1987-88
242	Coniel Norman	1972-73
237	Sean Elliott	1988-89
237	Anthony Cook	1988-89
235	Herman Harris	1976-77
231	Anthony Cook	1987-88
228	Ron Davis	1980-81

FIELD GOALS ATTEMPTED, SEASON

No.	Player	Year
572	Khalid Reeves	1993-94
528	Leon Blevins	1949-50
525	Coniel Norman	1973-74
520	Joe Skaisgir	1961-62
510	Herman Harris	1976-77
507	Bob Elliott	1974-75
494	Sean Elliott	1988-89
484	Damon Stoudamire	1993-94
476	Coniel Norman	1972-73
466	Damon Stoudamire	1994-95

FIELD GOAL PERCENTAGE, SEASON

Pct.	Player	Year
.676	Al Fleming	1973-74
.629	Anthony Cook	1988-89
.619	Brian Williams	1990-91
.618	Anthony Cook	1987-88
.607	Joseph Blair	1993-94
.607	Pete Williams	1984-85
.607	Jud Buechler	1988-89
.604	Pete Williams	1985-86
.599	Ed Stokes	1989-90
.598	Sean Rooks	1988-89

3-POINT FIELD GOAL PERCENTAGE, SEASON

(Minimum 40 attempts)

Pct.	Player	Years	3FGM-A
.573	Steve Kerr	1987-88	114-199
.483	Chris Mills	1992-1993	56-116
.475	Harvey Mason	1987-88	19-40
.471	Sean Elliott	1987-88	41-87
.465	Damon Stoudamire	1994-95	112-241
.463	Khalid Reeves	1990-91	31-67
.449	Matt Othick	1991-92	71-158
.446	Miles Simon	1994-95	29-65
.437	Sean Elliott	1988-89	66-151
.434	Matt Muehlebach	1989-90	66-152

3-PONT FIELD GOALS MADE, SEASON

No.	Player	Year
114	Steve Kerr	1987-88
112	Damon Stoudamire	1994-95
93	Damon Stoudamire	1993-94
85	Khalid Reeves	1993-94
71	Matt Othick	1991-92
68	Craig McMillan	1986-87
66	Matt Muehlebach	1989-90
66	Sean Elliott	1988-89
56	Chris Mills	1992-93
48	Matt Othick	1990-91

3-POINT FIELD GOALS ATTEMPTED, SEASON

No.	Player	Year
265	Damon Stoudamire	1993-94
241	Damon Stoudamire	1994-95
224	Khalid Reeves	1993-94
199	Steve Kerr	1987-88
160	Craig McMillan	1986-87
158	Matt Othick	1991-92
152	Matt Muehlebach	1989-90
151	Sean Elliott	1988-89
134	Matt Othick	1990-91
128	Matt Othick	1989-90

FREE THROWS, SEASON

No.	Player	Year
211	Khalid Reeves	1993-94
195	Sean Elliott	1988-89
177	Ernie McCray	1959-60
176	Sean Elliott	1987-88
152	Eddie Smith	1984-85
151	Tom Tolbert	1987-88
145	Bob Elliott	1975-76
144	Al Fleming	1974-75
140	Sean Rooks	1991-92
131	Ed Nymeyer	1955-56

FREE THROWS ATTEMPTED, SEASON

No.	Player	Year
264	Khalid Reeves	1993-94
257	Ernie McCray	1959-60
232	Sean Elliott	1988-89
225	Bob Elliott	1975-76
222	Sean Elliott	1987-88
215	Sean Rooks	1991-92
208	Bob Elliott	1974-75
197	Eddie Smith	1984-85
187	Bill Warner	1970-71
186	Tom Tolbert	1987-88

FREE THROW PERCENTAGE, SEASON

(Minimum 2.0 made per game)

Pct.	Player	Year
.891	Dylan Rigdon	1993-94
.885	Joe Nehls	1979-80
.859	Bob Spahn	1965-66
.855	Mickey Foster	1969-70
.841	Sean Elliott	1988-89
.836	Chris Mills	1992-93
.833	Mickey Foster	1968-69
.832	Warren Rustand	1965-66
.829	Coniel Norman	1972-73
.826	Damon Stoudamire	1994-95

REBOUNDS, SEASON

No.	Player	Year
373	Leo Johnson	1950-51
343	Al Fleming	1974-75
	Bill Reeves	1955-56
341	Bob Elliott	1975-76
329	Al Fleming	1975-76
314	Joe Skaisgir	1961-62
292	Phil Taylor	1976-77
290	Ernie McCray	1959-60
286	Albert Johnson	1963-64
285	Ray Owes	1993-94

REBOUND AVERAGE, SEASON

Average	Player	Year
13.2	Bill Reeves	1955-56
12.5	Leo Johnson	1950-51
12.2	Ernie McCray	1959-60
12.1	Joe Skaisgir	1961-62
11.8	Al Fleming	1974-75
11.0	Albert Johnson	1963-64
10.8	Phil Taylor	1976-77
10.7	Bill Reeves	1956-57
	Ernie McCray	1957-58
	Bob Elliott	1973-74

SCORERS, INDIVIDUAL

1. Sean Elliott

Year	Games	FGM-A	FG%	3FGM-A	3FG%	FTM-A	FT%	PTS	AVG.
1985-86	32	187-385	.486	-	-	127-167	.760	499	15.6
1986-87	30	209-410	.510	33-89	.371	127-165	.770	578	19.3
1987-88	38	263-461	.570	41-87	.471	176-222	.793	743	19.6
1988-89	33	237-494	.480	66-151	.437	195-232	.841	735	22.3
Career	133	896-1,750	.512	140-327	.428	625-786	.795	2,555	19.2

2. Bob Elliott

Year	G	FGM-A	FG%	FTM-A	FT%	PTS	Avg.
1973-74	26	158-323	.489	113-157	.720	429	16.5
1974-75	29	273-507	.538	131-208	.630	677	23.3
1975-76	33	225-406	.554	145-225	.644	595	18.0
1976-77	26	152-276	.551	126-177	.712	430	16.5
Career	114	808-1,512	.534	515-767	.671	2,125	18.6

3. Khalid Reeves

Year	Games	FGM-A	FG%	3FGM-A	3FG%	FTM-A	FT%	PTS	AVG.
1990-91	35	104-229	.454	31-67	.463	78-113	.690	317	9.1
1991-92	30	148-311	.476	44-119	.370	78-99	.788	418	13.9
1992-93	28	118-237	.498	26-79	.329	80-110	.727	342	12.2
1993-94	35	276-572	.483	85-224	.379	211-264	.799	848	24.2
Career	128	646-1,349	.479	186-489	.380	447-586	.763	1,925	15.0

4. Damon Stoudamire

Year	Games	FGM-A	FG%	3FGM-A	3FG%	FTM-A	FT%	PTS	AVG.
1991-92	30	76-167	.455	28-69	.406	37-48	.771	217	7.2
1992-93	28	99-226	.438	39-102	.382	72-91	.791	309	11.0
1993-94	35	217-484	.448	93-265	.351	112-140	.800	639	18.3
1994-95	30	222-466	.476	112-241	.465	128-155	.826	684	22.8
Career	123	614-1,343	.457	272-677	.402	349-434	.804	1,849	15.0

5. Al Fleming

Year	G	FGM-A	FG%	FTM-A	FT%	PTS	AVG
1972-73	26	130-242	.537	74-98	.755	334	12.8
1973-74	26	136-204	.667	58-78	.744	330	12.7
1974-75	29	215-381	.564	144-194	.742	574	19.8
1975-76	33	207-354	.586	113-152	.743	527	16.0
Career	114	688-1,181	.583	389-462	.842	1,765	15.5

6. Chris Mills

Year	Games	FGM-A	FG%	3FGM-A	3FG%	FTM-A	FT%	PTS	AVG.
1990-91	35	206-397	.519	42-122	.344	91-122	.746	545	15.6
1991-92	31	198-391	.506	28-89	.315	80-103	.777	504	16.3
1992-93	28	211-406	.520	56-116	.483	92-110	.836	570	20.4
Career	94	615-834	.737	126-327	.385	263-335	.785	1,619	17.2

7. Anthony Cook

Year	Games	FGM-A	FG%	3FGM-A	3FG%	FTM-A	FT%	PTS	AVG.
1985-86	32	73-146	.500	-	-	48-73	.658	194	6.1
1986-87	30	118-246	.480	0-0	.000	54-100	.540	290	9.7
1987-88	38	201-325	.618	0-1	.000	126-176	.716	528	13.9
1988-89	33	237-377	.629	0-1	.000	104-166	.627	578	17.5
Career	133	629-1,094	.575	0-2	.000	332-515	.645	1,590	12.0

8. Sean Rooks

Year	Games	FGM-A	FG%	3FGM-A	3FG%	FTM-A	FT%	PTS	AVG.
1988-89	32	70-117	.598	0-0	.000	40-65	.615	180	5.6
1989-90	31	140-263	.532	0-0	.000	114-161	.708	394	12.7
1990-91	35	159-283	.562	2-4	.500	98-149	.654	418	11.9
1991-92	31	181-323	.560	3-5	.600	140-215	.651	505	16.3
Career	129	550-986	.558	5-9	.556	392-590	.664	1,497	11.6

9. Bill Warner

Year	Games	FGM-A	FG%	FTM-A	FT%	PTS	AVG
1968-69	26	157-359	.438	76-111	.685	390	15.0
1969-70	26	216-445	.485	97-130	.746	529	20.3
1970-71	26	209-459	.455	125-187	.668	543	20.9
Career	78	582-1,263	.461	298-428	.696	1,462	18.7

10. Steve Kerr

Year	Games	FGM-A	FG%	3FGM-A	3FG%	FTM-A	FT%	PTS	AVG.
1983-84	28	81-157	.516	-	-	36-52	.692	198	7.1
1984-85	31	126-222	.568	-	-	57-71	.803	309	10.0
1985-86	32	195-361	.540	-	-	71-79	.899	461	14.4
1987-88	38	151-270	.559	114-199	.573	61-74	.824	477	12.6
Career	129	553-1,010	.548	114-199	.573	225-276	.815	1,445	11.2

1,000 POINTS ANYBODY

Players with 1,000 or more points in a career

Rank/Player	Years	Games	FG	FT	Points	Avg.
1. Sean Elliott	1986-89	133	896	623	2,555	190.2
2. Bob Elliott	1974-77	114	808	515	2,131	18.7
3. Khalid Reeves	1991-94	128	646	447	1,925	15.0
4. Damon Stoudamire	1992-95	126	614	349	1,849	15.0
5. Al Fleming	1973-76	114	688	389	1,765	15.5
6. Chris Mills	1991-93	94	615	263	1,619	17.2
7. Anthony Cook	1986-89	133	629	332	1,590	12.0
8. Sean Rooks	1988-92	129	550	392	1,497	11.6
9. Bill Warner	1969-71	78	582	298	1,462	18.7
10. Steve Kerr	1984-88	139	553	225	1,445	10.4
11. Joe Nehls	1976-80	84	569	271	1,409	16.8
12. Ernie McCray	1958-60	76	510	329	1,349	17.8
13. Frank Smith	1980-83	109	530	269	1,329	12.2
14. Link Richmond	1943-49	118	525	196	1,246	10.6
15. Ed Nymeyer	1956-58	78	437	351	1,225	15.7
16. Coniel Norman	1973-74	50	506	182	1,194	23.9
17. Ray Owes	1992-95	120	459	228	1,178	9.8
18. Craig McMillan	1985-88	140	414	211	1,174	8.4
19. Herman Harris	1974-77	93	521	116	1,158	12.5
20. Jud Buechler	1987-90	131	439	226	1,144	8.7
21. Phil Taylor	1975-78	106	482	163	1,127	11.1
22. Matt Othick	1989-92	129	298	268	1,055	8.2
23. Roger Johnson	1950-53	85	401	244	1,046	12.3
24. Joe Skaisgir	1961-62	52	407	220	1,034	13.3
25. Albert Johnson	1963-65	78	391	252	1,034	13.3
26. Matt Muehlebach	1988-91	128	322	199	1,006	7.9

800 POINT PLATEAU IN SEASON

Year	Player	Games	FG	FT	Pts	Avg.
1993-94	Khalid Reeves	35	276	211	848	24.2

700 POINT PLATEAU IN SEASON

Year	Player	Games	FG	FT	Pts	Avg.
1987-88	Sean Elliott	38	263	176	743	19.6
1988-89	Sean Elliott	33	237	195	735	22.2

600 POINT PLATEAU IN SEASON

Year	Player	Games	FG	FT	Pts	Avg.
1994-95	Damon Stoudamire	30	222	128	684	22.8
1974-75	Bob Elliott	29	273	131	677	23.3
1993-94	Damon Stoudamire	35	217	112	639	18.3
1973-74	Coniel Norman	26	264	90	618	23.8

500 POINT PLATEAU IN SEASON

Year	Player	Games	FG	FT	Pts	Avg.
1975-76	Bob Elliott	33	225	145	595	18.0
1988-89	Anthony Cook	33	237	104	578	17.5
1986-87	Sean Elliott	30	209	127	578	19.3
1972-73	Coniel Norman	24	242	92	576	24.0
1974-75	Al Fleming	29	215	144	574	19.8
1959-60	Ernie McCray	24	198	177	573	23.9
1992-93	Chris Mills	28	211	92	570	20.4
1990-91	Chris Mills	35	206	91	545	15.6
1976-77	Herman Harris	27	235	73	543	20.0
1970-71	Bill Warner	26	209	125	543	20.9
1987-88	Tom Tolbert	38	192	151	536	14.1
1980-81	Ron Davis	27	228	73	529	19.6
1969-70	Bill Warner	26	216	97	529	20.3
1961-62	Joe Skaisgir	26	208	113	529	20.3
1987-88	Anthony Cook	38	201	126	528	13.9
1975-76	Al Fleming	33	207	113	527	16.0
1979-80	Joe Nehls	27	207	108	522	19.3
1978-79	Larry Demic	27	213	96	522	19.3
1978-79	Joe Nehls	27	203	109	519	19.1
1960-61	Joe Skaisgir	26	199	107	505	19.4
1991-92	Sean Rooks	31	181	140	505	16.3
1991-92	Chris Mills	31	198	80	504	16.3
1984-85	Eddie Smith	31	174	152	500	16.1

YEARLY LEADERS

SCORING LEADERS

Year	Player	Games	FG	FT	PTS	AVG.
1995-96	Ben Davis	33	171	127	469	14.2
1994-95	Damon Stoudamire	30	222	128	684	22.8
1993-94	Khalid Reeves	35	276	211	848	24.2
1992-93	Chris Mills	28	211	92	570	20.4
1991-92	Sean Rooks	31	181	140	505	16.3
1990-91	Chris Mills	35	206	91	545	15.6
1989-90	Jud Buechler	32	182	88	477	14.9
1988-89	Sean Elliott	33	237	195	735	22.2
1987-88	Sean Elliott	38	263	176	743	19.6
1986-87	Sean Elliott	30	209	127	578	19.3
1985-86	Sean Elliott	32	187	127	499	15.6
1984-85	Eddie Smith	31	174	152	500	16.1
1983-84	Pete Williams	28	151	105	407	14.5
1982-83	Frank Smith	28	148	88	384	13.7
1981-82	Greg Cook	27	344	160	392	14.5
1980-81	Ron Davis	27	228	73	529	19.6
1979-80	Joe Nehls	27	207	108	522	19.3
1978-79	Larry Demic	27	213	96	522	19.3
1977-78	Phil Taylor	26	185	62	432	16.6
1976-77	Herman Harris	27	235	73	510	20.0
1975-76	Bob Elliott	33	225	145	595	18.0
1974-75	Bob Elliott	29	273	131	677	23.3
1973-74	Coniel Norman	26	264	90	618	23.8
1972-73	Coniel Norman	24	242	92	576	24.0
1971-72	Jim Huckestein	26	182	87	451	17.3
1970-71	Bill Warner	26	209	125	543	20.9

Year	Player	Games	FG	FT	PTS	AVG.
1969-70	Bill Warner	26	216	97	529	20.3
1968-69	Bill Warner	26	157	76	390	15.0
1967-68	Bill Davis	24	161	99	421	17.5
1966-67	Bill Davis	25	141	102	284	15.4
1965-66	Ted Prickett	26	154	121	429	16.5
1964-65	Warren Rustand	26	137	94	368	14.2
1963-64	Albert Johnson	26	157	81	395	15.2
1962-63	Albert Johnson	26	125	86	336	12.9
1961-62	Joe Skaisgir	26	205	113	529	20.3
1960-61	Joe Skaisgir	26	199	107	505	19.4
1959-60	Ernie McCray	24	198	177	573	23.9
1958-59	Ernie McCray	26	174	66	414	15.9
1957-58	Ed Nymeyer	26	146	116	408	15.7
1956-57	Ed Nymeyer	26	153	104	410	15.7
1955-56	Ed Nymeyer	26	138	131	407	15.6
1954-55	Hadie Redd	25	110	119	339	13.6
1953-54	Hadie Redd	24	118	80	316	13.2
1952-53	Bill Kemmeries	26	116	127	359	13.8
1951-52	Bill Kemmeries	27	150	89	389	14.1
1950-51	Bob Honea	30	152	81	385	12.8
1949-50	Leon Blevins	31	185	92	462	14.9
1948-49	Leon Blevins	28	156	78	390	13.5
1947-48	Morris Udall	28	153	65	371	13.2
1946-47	Linc Richmond	24	180	68	428	17.9
1945-46	Linc Richmond	21	130	52	312	14.8
1944-45	Jimmy Steele	18	90	37	217	12.1
1943-44	George Genung	13	76	25	177	13.6
1942-43	Bob Ruman	22	101	38	240	11.4
1941-42	Vince Cullen	22	109	10	228	10.4
1940-41	Vince Cullen	18	94	10	198	11.0
1939-40	George Jordan	25	97	37	231	9.2
1938-39	George Jordan	22	78	35	191	8.7
1937-38	Lorry DiGrazia	21	85	41	211	10.0
1936-37	Lorry DiGrazia	25	91	27	209	8.4
1935-36	Lorry DiGrazia	23	81	29	191	8.3
1934-35	Walt Scholtzhauer	17	88	21	197	11.6
1933-34	Vince Byrne	27	104	68	276	10.2
1932-33	Jack Raffety	23	81	20	182	7.9
1931-32	Howard Abbott	20	97	29	223	11.2
1930-31	Jack Raffety	9	44	10	98	10.9
1929-30	Neal Goodman	21	78	29	175	8.4
1928-29	Neal Goodman	23	96	29	221	9.6
1927-28	Larry Edwards	14	51	9	111	7.9
1926-27	Charles Miller	16	55	32	142	8.9
1925-26	Byron Drachman	13	-	-	117	9.0
1924-25	Clarence Skousen	11	-	-	92	8.4
1923-24	Harold Tovrea	17	133	28	294	17.3
1922-23	Harold Tovrea	20	-	-	316	15.8
1921-22	A.L. Slonaker	8	-	-	140	7.5
1920-21	A.L. Slonaker	7	-	-	163	23.7

REBOUNDING LEADERS

Year	Player	Games	RBS	AVG.
1995-96	Ben Davis	33	313	9.5
1994-95	Ray Owes	31	252	8.1
1993-94	Ray Owes	35	285	8.1
1992-93	Chris Mills	28	222	7.9
1991-92	Chris Mills	31	244	7.9
1990-91	Brian Williams	35	273	7.8
1989-90	Jud Buechler	32	264	8.3
1988-89	Anthony Cook	33	238	7.2
1987-88	Anthony Cook	38	269	7.1
1986-87	Anthony Cook	30	217	7.2
1985-86	John Edgar	32	237	7.3
1984-85	Pete Williams	31	265	8.5
1983-84	Pete Williams	28	278	9.9
1982-83	Frank Smith	28	212	7.6
1981-82	Frank Smith	27	205	7.8
1980-81	Robbie Dosty	27	178	6.6
1979-80	Frank Smith	27	162	6.0
1978-79	Larry Demic	27	277	10.3
1977-78	Phil Taylor	26	210	8.1
1976-77	Phil Taylor	27	292	10.8
1975-76	Bob Elliott	33	341	10.3
1974-75	Al Fleming	29	343	11.8
1973-74	Bob Elliott	26	278	10.7
1972-73	Al Fleming	26	257	9.9
1971-72	Lynard Harris	26	245	9.4
1970-71	Eddie Myers	26	239	9.2
1969-70	Tom Lee	26	258	9.9
1968-69	Eddie Myers	27	279	10.3
1967-68	Bill Davis	24	253	10.6
1966-67	Bill Davis	25	192	7.7
1965-66	Mike Aboud	26	219	8.4
1964-65	Albert Johnson	26	234	9.0
1963-64	Albert Johnson	26	286	11.0
1962-63	Albert Johnson	26	253	9.7
1961-62	Joe Skaisgir	26	314	12.1
1960-61	Joe Skaisgir	26	268	10.3

TOP FIELD GOAL PERCENTAGE BY YEAR

Year	Player	FGM	FGA	Pct.
1995-96	Joseph Blair	89	129	.690
1994-95	Joseph Blair	142	254	.559
1993-94	Joseph Blair	153	252	.607
1992-93	Chris Mills	211	406	.520
1991-92	Sean Rooks	181	323	.560
1990-91	Brian Williams	195	315	.619
1989-90	Ed Stokes	94	157	.599
1988-89	Anthony Cook	237	377	.629
1987-88	Anthony Cook	201	325	.618
1986-87	Tom Tolbert	156	305	.511
1985-86	Steve Kerr	195	361	.540
1984-85	Pete Williams	145	239	.607
1983-84	Pete Williams	151	250	.604
1982-83	Frank Smith	148	282	.535
1981-82	Frank Smith	156	275	.587
1980-81	Frank Smith	123	230	.535
1979-80	Ron Davis	136	269	.506
1978-79	Larry Demic	213	373	.571
1977-78	Joe Nehls	159	313	.508
1976-77	Bob Elliott	152	276	.551
1975-76	Al Fleming	207	354	.585
1974-75	Al Fleming	215	381	.564
1973-74	Al Fleming	136	269	.506
1972-73	Al Fleming	130	242	.537
1971-72	Lynard Harris	125	256	.488
1970-71	Tom Lee	144	292	.493
1969-70	Bill Warner	216	445	.485
1968-69	Tom Lee	122	239	.468
1967-68	Bill Davis	161	313	.514
1966-67	Bill Davis	141	302	.467
1965-66	Ted Prickett	154	312	.493
1964-65	Warren Rustand	137	372	.504
1963-64	Warren Rustand	120	275	.436
1962-63	Warren Rustand	99	219	.452
1961-62	Joe Skaisgir	208	520	.400
1960-61	Joe Skaisgir	199	457	.435

TOP 3-POINT FG PERCENTAGE LEADERS

(Two attempts per team game played)

Year	Player	FGM	FGA	Pct.
1995-96	Joe McLean	50	119	.420
1994-95	Damon Stoudamire	112	241	.465
1993-94	Khalid Reeves	85	224	.379
1992-93	Chris Mills	56	116	.483
1991-92	Matt Othick	71	158	.449
1990-91	Khalid Reeves	31	67	.463
1989-90	Matt Muehlebach	66	152	.434
1988-89	Sean Elliott	66	152	.434
1987-88	Steve Kerr	114	199	.573
1986-87	Craig McMillan	68	160	.425

TOP FT PERCENTAGE LEADERS

Year	Player	FTM	FTA	Pct.
1995-96	Miles Simon	120	157	.764
1994-95	Damon Stoudamire	128	155	.826
1993-94	Dylan Rigdon	82	92	.891
1992-93	Chris Mills	92	110	.836
1991-92	Khalid Reeves	78	99	.788
1990-91	Matt Othick	77	98	.786
1989-90	Matt Muehlebach	62	76	.816
1988-89	Sean Elliott	195	232	.841
1987-88	Tom Tolbert	151	186	.812
1986-87	Sean Elliott	127	165	.770
1985-86	Steve Kerr	71	79	.899
1984-85	Eddie Smith	152	207	.734
1983-84	Eddie Smith	87	119	.731
1982-83	Brock Brunkhorst	48	63	.762
1981-82	Jack Magno	33	46	.717
1980-81	Robbie Dosty	64	81	.790
1979-80	Joe Nehls	108	122	.885
1978-79	Joe Nehls	109	133	.820
1977-78	Joe Nehls	50	58	.862

Year	Player	FTM	FTA	Pct.
1976-77	Herman Harris	73	96	.760
1975-76	Gilbert Myles	63	81	.778
1974-75	Len Gordy	48	61	.787
1973-74	Al Fleming	58	78	.744
1972-73	Coniel Norman	92	111	.829
1971-72	Jim Huckestein	87	113	.771
1970-71	Walt McKinney	57	67	.851
1969-70	Mickey Foster	100	117	.855
1968-69	Mickey Foster	85	102	.833
1967-68	Mickey Foster	59	77	.766
1966-67	Mike Welton	63	80	.788
1965-66	Bob Spahn	73	85	.859
1964-65	Warren Rustand	94	113	.832
1963-64	Warren Rustand	92	114	.807
1962-63	Warren Rustand	78	99	.788
1961-62	Joe Skaisgir	113	156	.718
1960-61	Mary Dutt	61	88	.693

ASSIST LEADERS

Year	Player	Games	Assists	Avg.
1995-96	Reggie Geary	33	231	7.0
1994-95	Damon Stoudamire	30	220	7.3
1993-94	Damon Stoudamire	35	208	5.9
1992-93	Damon Stoudamire	28	159	5.7
1991-92	Matt Othick	31	160	5.2
1990-91	Matt Othick	35	181	5.3
1989-90	Matt Muehlebach	32	181	5.3
1988-89	Ken Lofton	33	135	4.1
1987-88	Steve Kerr	38	150	3.9
1986-87	Sean Elliott	30	110	3.7
1985-86	Steve Kerr	38	150	3.8
1984-85	Brock Brunkhorst	25	130	5.2
1983-84	Brock Brunkhorst	28	98	3.5
1982-83	Brock Brunkhorst	26	120	4.6
1981-82	Ricky Walker	20	65	3.3
1980-81	Rusell Brown	27	166	6.1
1979-80	Russell Brown	27	200	7.4
1978-79	Russell Brown	27	247	9.1
1977-78	Russell Brown	26	197	7.6
1976-77	Gary Harrison	27	128	4.7
1975-76	Jim Rappis	31	105	3.5
1974-75	Gilbert Myles	26	136	5.5
1973-74	Eric Money	20	110	5.5
1972-73	Eric Money	26	96	3.7
1951-52	Roger Johnson	27	86	3.2
1950-51	Leo Johnson	30	146	4.9

BLOCKED SHOTS LEADERS

Year	Player	Games	Blocks	Avg.
1995-96	Reggie Geary	33	24	0.72
1994-95	Joseph Blair	28	31	1.1
1993-94	Joseph Blair	35	37	1.1
1992-93	Ed Stokes	28	37	1.3
1991-92	Ed Stokes	31	41	1.3
1990-91	Sean Rooks	35	43	1.2
1989-90	Ed Stokes	29	49	1.7
1988-89	Anthony Cook	33	84	2.5
1987-88	Anthony Cook	38	75	2.0
1986-87	Anthony Cook	30	69	2.3
1985-86	Anthony Cook	32	50	1.6
1984-85	Pete Williams	31	21	0.7
1983-84	Pete Williams	28	20	0.7
1982-83	Frank Smith	28	23	0.8
1981-82	Frank Smith	27	25	0.9
1980-81	Frank Smith	27	20	0.7
1979-80	Frank Smith	27	16	0.6
1978-79	Larry Demic	27	22	0.8
1977-78	Larry Demic	26	42	1.6
1976-77	Bob Elliott	26	29	1.1
1975-76	Bob Elliott	27	16	0.6

Year	Player	Games	Steals	Avg.
1995-96	Reggie Geary	33	67	2.0
1994-95	Damon Stoudamire	30	52	1.7
1993-94	Khalid Reeves	35	64	1.8
1992-93	Damon Stoudamire	28	45	1.6
1991-92	Khalid Reeves	30	50	1.7
1990-91	Matt Muehlebach	35	58	1.7
1989-90	Matt Muehlbach	32	41	1.3
1988-89	Ken Lofton	33	67	2.0
1987-88	Ken Lofton	38	60	1.6
1986-87	Ken Lofton	30	55	1.8

Year	Player	Games	Steals	Avg.
1985-86	Steve Kerr	32	52	1.6
1984-85	Eddie Smith	31	37	1.2
1983-84	Eddie Smith	28	46	1.6
1982-83	Puntus Wilson	28	44	1.6
1981-82	Greg Cook	27	43	1.6
1980-81	John Smith	27	48	1.8
1979-80	Russell Brown	27	46	1.7
1978-79	Russell Brown	27	50	1.9
1977-78	Russell Brown	26	38	1.5
1976-77	Herman Harris	27	45	1.7
1975-76	Herman Harris	27	34	1.3

HONORS

PLAYER OF THE YEAR

1988-89 Sean Elliott, Consensus

ALL-AMERICANS

1950-51 Roger Johnson (third, Helms Foundation)
1975-76 Bob Elliott (third, Basketball Weekly)
1976-77 Bob Elliott (HF/CC)
1987-88 Sean Elliott (Consensus); Steve Kerr, (2nd, Associated Press; 3rd, NABC)
1990-91 Chris Mills, Brian Williams (AP, honorable mention)
1991-92 Chris Mills, Sean Rooks (AP honorable mention)
1992-93 Chris Mills (2nd, Basketball Weekly; third, Basketball Times, NABC, AP, UPI)
1993-94 Khalid Reeves (first, John Wooden; second, AP, Sporting News, USBWA, Basketball Weekly; third, NABC); Damon Stoudamire (honorable mention, AP, Basketball Weekly, USBWA)
1994-95 Damon Stoudamire (Consensus)

ALL-PACIFIC-10 CONFERENCE

1978-79 Larry Demic; Joe Nehls (second); Russell Brown (honorable mention)
1979-80 Joe Nehls
1980-81 Ron Davis
1981-82 Frank Smith (honorable mention)
1983-84 Pete Williams
1984-85 Pete Williams; Eddie Smith; Brock Brunkhorst
1985-86 Steve Kerr
1986-87 Sean Elliott
1987-88 Sean Elliott (MVP); Steve Kerr; Anthony Cook
1988-89 Sean Elliott (MVP); Anthony Cook
1989-90 Jud Buechler
1990-91 Brian Williams
1991-92 Chris Mills; Sean Rooks
1992-93 Chris Mills (MVP); Damon Stoudamire
1993-94 Khalid Reeves; Damon Stoudamire
1994-95 Damon Stoudamire (co-MVP); Ray Owes; Joseph Blair (honorable mention)
1995-96 Reggie Geary; Ben Davis

ALL-WESTERN ATHLETIC CONFERENCE

1962-63 Warren Rustand (second); Albert Johnson (second)
1963-64 Warren Rustand; Albert Johnson (second)
1964-65 Warren Rustand; Albert Johnson (second)
1965-66 Ted Prickett (second)
1967-68 Bill Davis
1969-70 Bill Warner (second)
1970-71 Bill Warner (second)

1971-72 Jim Huckestein (second)
1972-73 Coniel Norman; Eric Money (second)
1973-74 Coniel Norman; Al Fleming (second); Eric Money (second)
1974-75 Al Fleming; Bob Elliott
1975-76 Al Fleming; Bob Elliott; Jim Rappis (second)
1976-77 Bob Elliott; Herman Harris
1977-78 Phil Taylor (second)

ALL-BORDER CONFERENCE

1933-34 Vince Byrne; Gene Filbrun; George Johnson
1934-35 Walter Scholtzhauer; Ralph Winters (second)
1935-36 Lory DiGrazia; Morion Coltrin; Elmer Vickers
1936-37 Lory DiGrazia; Marion Coltrin
1937-38 Lory DeGrazia; Tom Greenfield
1938-39 Carl Berra
1939-40 Wimer Harper (second); Carl Berra (second); George Jordan (second); Stewart Udall (second)
1940-41 Wilmer Harper (second); Vince Cullem (second); Don Gatchel (second)
1941-42 Bob Ruman (second)
1942-43 Vince Cullem; Bob Ruman (second); Marv Borodkin (second)
1945-46 Linc Richmond; Tim Ballantyne; Marv Borodkin (second); George Genung (second)
1946-47 Linc Richmond; Fred Enke; Junior Crum; Marv Borodkin
1947-48 Morris Udall; Fred Enke; Bill Mann
1948-49 Leon Blevins; Hillard Crum (second)
1949-50 Leon Blevins; Roger Johnson; Bob Honea (second); Leo Johnson (second)
1950-51 Bob Honea; Roger Johnson; Leo Johnson; Dave Schuff (second)
1951-52 Bill Kemmeries (second)
1953-54 Hadie Redd (second); John Bruner (second)
1954-55 Hadie Redd (second)
1955-56 Ed Nymeyer (second)
1956-57 Bob Mueller; Ed Nymeyer (second)
1957-58 Ed Nymeyer (second)
1958-59 Ernie McCray (second)
1959-60 Ernie McCray; Jon Conner (second)
1960-61 Joe Skaisgir (second)

LETTERMEN

A Howard Abbot, 1932-34; Michael Aboud 1965-67; Dennis Albright 1963, 1965; Robert Aleksa 1975-76; Ronald S. Allen 1973-74; Thomas R. Allin 1941-42; Bruce D. Anderson 1970-72; Warren A. Anderson 1970.

B Cecil Eugene Baldwin 1957; Thomas M. Ballantyne 1942-44, 1946-47; Sam Balsley 1965-66; John D. Barkley 1956; Marty Barmentloo 1995; Richard L. Barnes 1970; James T. Barrett 1912; John B. Barringer 1936-37; Kendrick A. Bartheis 1936; Charles Beach 1913; John M. Belobraydic 1979-81, 1983; Craig Bergman 1988; Robert H. Berman 1918; Carl Berra 1938-40; John Biggs 1935; Hugo Ernest Birkner 1907; John Russell Black, 1939-41; William Thomas Black 1944; Ernest O. Blades 1907-10; Joseph J. Blair 1993-96; James Darrell Blankinship 1955; Leon G. Blevins 1949-50; Edward Bliss 1926; Edrick Bohannon 1993; George Vance Booker 1923; Marvin Borodkin 1942-43, 1946-47; Harold Bowen 1924; Richard Brackenbury 1916-17; Hubert Bradford 1905; Roger Brautigan 1966; Wm. D. Breck 1962-64; James A. Brittain 1959; Forrest Ronald Broadwater 1932; Paul C. Brooke 1917; Eddie E. Brooke 1927; Kenneth Brooks 1968-69, Frank A. Brookshier 1924-27; James E. Brower 1953-55, Andy Brown 1994; Charles Owen Brown, Jr. 1905-06; J. Duncan Brown 1927; Lawrence A. Brown 1954; Roger Brown 1918; Russell K. Brown 1978-1981; John M. Bruner 1952-54; Brock Brunkhorst 1982-85; Jud D. Buechler 1987-90; David J. Burns 1974-75; Julius Ralph Bush 1918; Horatio Cotter Butts 1926; Vincent R. Byrne 1932-34.

C Clarence R. Capps 1945; Arthur Carroll 1949, 1951; Travis J. Case 1951, 1953; Joe Wesley Cherry 1947-49; Marshall Christy 1933; Marvin Carl Clark 1923-25; Dan W. Clarke 1937-39; Monte C. Clausen 1961-63; Phillip Clemeons 1919; Leo Fredrick Cloud 1911-15; Horace Merle Cochran 1912-13; Jeff Collins 1981; Marion J. Coltrin 1936-37; Jon C. Conner 1958-60; Joseph W. Conway 1919; Raymond W. Conway 1937-39; Anthony L. Cook 1986-89; Charles E. Cooke 1964; Greg Cook 1982; Troy Cooke 1983-84; Eric E. Cooper 1986; Leander Cox, Jr. 1938, 1940; Terence M. Coyle 1955-57; Jon A. Crawford 1959; Edgar T. Crismon 1931, 1933; Cecil James Crouch 1948, 1950; Robert E. Crouch 1925-27; Hillard H. Crum, Jr. 1946-49; Albert Vincent Cellen, 1941-43; John Harding Culin 1907-08; Ron Curry 1989; John F. Cushman 1956.

D Edward F. Daasch 1963-65; Alonzo Lee Danley 1937-39; Regis A. Dauk 1961-63; Brian L. David 1987-90; Ben Davis 1995-96; Frank Davis 1934-35; Ronald D. Davis 1980-81; William D. Davis 1967-68; William Kenny Davis 1977-78; Wm. J. Decker 1962; Salvatore J. DeFrancesco 1955; Larry Demic 1976-79; Richard Dermody 1942-44; Michael Dickerson 1995-96; Waldo M. Dicus 1928-30; Theodore R. Diebold 1927; M. Morry DiGrazia 1936-38; Jerome Dillon 1951-52; Raymond E. Donnelly 1979-80; Tom Donovan 1943; Edward W. Doolen 1963-65; Robbie D. Dosty 1978-81; James Perry Doyle 1919; Byron C. Drachman 1926; Melvyn Drucker 1960; James E. Dunlap 1950, 1952-53; Marvin Alvin Dutt 1960-61; Heman A. Duwe 1934-35.

E Kelvin Eafon 1995-96; Randall E. Echols 1973; Jackson R. Eddy 1953-54; John Edgar 1985-86; Ambrose Earl Edgarton 1907-08; Lawrence Edwards 1928; Philip C. Edwards 1971-73; Thomas Ehlmann 1975; William David Elder 1946; Lloyd Creighton Elliott 1911, 1913; Robert A. Elliott 1974-77; Sean M. Elliott 1986-89; Fred William Enke 1946-48; Ken Ensor 1983-84; James F. Eppler 1956-57; J. Fred Erdhaus 1939; Larry Douglas Ewald 1958.

F Richard R. Farman 1962; Webster L. Fickett 1914; Davis Eugene Filbrun 1932-34; William Lindsey Flake 1940-41; Kevin T. Flanagan 1991-94; John B. Flannery 1954; Al Fleming, Jr. 1973-76; Wesley T. Flynn 1961-63; Joyce Forbes 1962; Michael E. Foster

1968-70; Harvey B. Fox 1964-66; Bruce T. Fraser 1985-87; Ronald Fuller 1976.

G Rudolph R. Garcia 1962; L. Scott Gardner 1972; Donald G. Gatchel 1940-41; Reggie E. Geary 1993-96; Jay L. Geldmacher 1974; Barry Genesen 1964; George Farrell Genung 1942-44, 1946-47; Frank Tom Gibblings 1924, 1926; Alvan Cullam Gillem Jr. 1907-08; Gerald A. Gitles 1952; Jerome C. Gladney 1974-77; Joseph Henry Glennon 1913; Lionel H. Goar 1956-57; Leon O. Goar 1955; A. Harold Goodman 1945-46; Neil Nathaniel Goodman 1929-30; Gordon Austin Goodwin 1920-21; Leonard Gordy 1974-77; John O. Graham 1931; Harry J. Gray 1931; Bradley W. Greene 19677-68; George E. Greene 1949-50; Tom Guy Greenfield 1937-38; Rollin T. Gridley 1925-27; Stanley E. Grimes 1956; Warren Arthur Grossetta 1908-09.

H Robert Lakenan Hall 1944; Cox Ham 1940; James E. Hansen 1967-69; Robert L. Hansen 1964-66; John L. Harbour 1968-69; William Hargis 1930; Wilmer Eugene Harper 1939-41; Richard Harrington 1959-60; Herman B. Harris 1974-77; Lawrence R. Harris 1962-64; Lynard Harris 1972-73; Gary L. Harrison 1975-77; Minor Louis Hartman 1911; David Haskin 1983-86; Burrell Richard Hatcher 1905, 1907; George N. Hawthorne 1979-80; Normal Clifton Hayhurst 1912-14; Eddie Held 1938; Hugh Max Helm 1942-43; Walter M. Helm 1936-38; James Prugh Herndon 1917-19; John Cole Hobbs 1920, 1922-23; Robert L. Honea 1949-51; Robert Louis Hopkins 1957-59; Jack R. Howell 1954; James W. Huckestein 1971-72; William C. Hudak 1954, 1956; T. Gordon Hull 1924.

I David L. Inglis 1953, 1956; Wm. C. Irvine 1950; John L. Irving 1973; Albin Iselin 1918; Oscar H. Islas 1952, 1954.

J William Christian Jack 1934; George Dewar Jackson 1936-38; Keith Jackson 1982-85; Gerald T. Jacobs 1965; Rolf A. Jacobs 1985-86; David Theodore Jacoby 1921; Albert J. Johnson 1963-65; Deron Johnson 1991-92; George Johnson 1932-34; Leo C. Johnson 1949-51; Roger E. Johnson 1950-52, Samuel H. Johnson 1936, 1938-39; James H. Johnston 1950; Mitchell E. Jones 1976, 1978; Percy Wonson Jones 1907; Robin Jones 1970-72; George Bernie Jones 1938-40; Robert C. Jordan 1960; Brian E. Jung 1976-77; Mark Junk 1982.

K Sidney L. Kain 1952-53; Steven M. Kanner 1975; Jarvis Kelley 1994-95; William F. Kemmeries 1951-53; Joe Kentz 1967-68, 1952-54; Steven D. Kerr 1984-88; Kevin Kinkade 1975; Michael W. Kordick 1968; Ken Joe Kurtz 1965.

L Leon Lampner 1945; Bruce Alan Larson 1949-50; Charles N. LaVetter 1964; Thomas O. Lavoy 1963-65; Thomas E. Lawson 1972-73; Arthur M. LaZar 1961; Eli Lazovich 1952-55; Thomas C. Lee 1969-71; N. Warner Lee 1959-60; Charles J. Leftault 1952-53; Henry Edward Leiber 1931; Charles Zaner Lesher 1916; Walter Coyle Lester 1924, 1926; John William Lewis 1905; E. Gordon Lindstrom 1967-68; Gregory Lloyd 1976; Bret Harlow Lockling 1920-22; Kenny Lofton 1986-89; John H. Low 1942-43; Earl R. Lubbers 1957; Balbo J. Lutich 1951; Cedric Lutz 1932.

Mc Patrick F. McAndrew 1966; Ernest C. McCray 1958-60; John Jacob McIntyre 1946, 1948; Walter McKinney 1969-71; Joseph R. McLean 1993-96; Craig S. McMillan 1985-88; Frank J. McSherry 1916-17.

M Francis C. Mack 1912-13, 15; James Stephen Maffeo 1914-1917; Jack Magno 1982; William Gibson Mann 1947-49; Chester L. Marsh 1925-26; Timothy D. Marshall 1976-78; Harvey J. Mason 1987-90; Adolph John Matulis 1941; Sylvester Maxey 1976; Robert E. Maxwell Jr. 1959; Donald E. Mellon 1980, 1982-83; Dean L. Metz; Leslie Creighton Millar 1908-10; Charles W. Miller 1925-27; Charles W. Miller 1980-82; John Robert Miller 1942-44; Christopher L. Mills

1991-93; Marcus Aurelius Smith Ming 1961; Lanny R. Mitchell 1970-71; Wm. Mitchell 1961; Richard L. Moe 1961; Eric V. Money 1973-74, Tony Leyva 1947-48, 1950; Lawrence Charles Morris 1917; David P. Mosebar 1980; Richard Lee Mower 1957-59; Matt Muehlebach 1988-91; Robert Louis Mueller 1956-58; Eddie M. Myers 1969-71; Gilbert Myles 1975-77.

N Raymond Lynn Naegle 1940; Joseph A. Nehls 1978-80; Myron Nelson 1929-31; John Newsome 1966-67; Spencer P. Nordyke 1930; Coniel Norman 1973-74; William H. Norris, Jr. 1972; Edward Fred Nymeyer 1956-58.

O William O'Donald 1955-57; Michael O'Haco 1941; James R. Oldham 1925; Ernest Oosterveen 1955-56; Matt Othick 1989-92; Ray Owes 1992-95.

P Roy Pace 1925; John Carlton Padelfrd Jr. 1943, 1947-48; Robert Palm 1935; Eugene V. Patten 1924; Harold A. Patten 1928-30; Paul H. Penner 1950; Charles Phillips Peterson 1945; Wiley K. Peterson 1928; David Peyton 1954; Wilford W. Phelps 1916-17; Theodis Pickett 1964-66; William Jacob Pistor 1919-22; Wm. E. Pitts 1954; George A. Ponsford 1932-34; Todd Porter 1983; William A. Porter 1915-16, Clair B. Preininger 1935; William M. Pryce 1928.

R Abe Rachim 1937; Jack Raffety 1931-32; James M. Rappis 1973-76; Ralph D. Reagor 1935; Duane Rebstock 1909-1911; Hadie Redd 1954-55; Milton L. Redfern 1927-28; Khalid Reeves 1991-1994; Robert William Reeves 1955-57; A.S. Reynolds 1948, 1950; Ralph Lyman Rhodes 1913-14; Raymond L. Rhodes 1948-49; William A. Rhodes 1958; Jason Richey 1994; Lincoln A. Richmond 1944, 46-49; Claude Lee Ricks Jr. 1947-48; Warren C. Ridge 1956-58; George Richard Ridgeway 1929-31; Dylan M. Rigdon 1993-94; John D. Riggs 1930; George B. Robertson 1909; Dwayne M. Robinson 1937; Abraham Rochlin 1937; Sean Lester Rooks 1989-92; Richard A. Root 1966-67; George Rountree 1953-55; Robert P. Ruman 1941-43; Warren S. Rustand 1963-65.

S Jose Urbano Salazar 1907-08, 1910; Frank Sancet 1929; Wm. Michael Schlebaum 1958; Casey Schmidt 1990-91; Walter S. Scholtzhauer 1935-36; David A. Schuff 1951; Greg Scott 1983; Dan A. Scurlock 1961; James G. Seal 1959; Kenneth Garland Seigle 1937, 1939; Alm Preston Sessions 1913-16; Tom R. Shoemaker 1951; Elias Sieger 1948; Louis Silverstein 1944, 1946; Miles Simon 1995-96; George Keith Sirrine 1945; Joseph G. Skaisgir 1961-62; Clarence Skousen 1925; Alter L. Slonaker 1918-20; Eugene E. Smallwood 1951; Clarence

J. Smith, Jr. 1951; Eddie Smith 1984-85; Frank H. Smith, Jr. 1980-83; John A. Smith 1978-81; William R. Smitheran 1953-54; George Sorenson 1927-29; James Souter 1958-59; Robert G. Spahn 1964-66; George Frederick Spaulding 1911; Roland A. Stamps 1968; Allan Jaynes Stanton 1951-52; James Charles Steele 1945; Russell L. Stevens 1960-61; Sam S. Stevens 1946; Jesse Hobson Stewart 1905; Ed K. Stokes 1990-93; Damon Stoudamire 1992-95; J. Donald Strigel 1928-30; Leon Henri Strong 1909; Paul A. Strong 1972-73; James Daniel Sullivan 1912; Tom Sutton 1966; Mitchell Swick-Vialo 1930.

T Michael Tait 1984; Greg Taylor 1983; Morgan Taylor 1983, 1985; Philip E. Taylor 1975-78; Raymond W. Tewksbury 1931; Robert Russell Thomas 1921-24; Austin Thomason 1931; Arthur Perry Thompson 1908; Byron Thomas Tolbert 1987-88; Harvey Thompson 1982-84; Harold Charles Tovrea 1921-24; J. Howard Tovrea 1928; William T. Trask 1970; James M. Treat 1972; Richard Triniman 1923; Maurice Kenneth Troutt 1949-50; Andrew Jack Troutz 1946; Irvong F. Truman 1913-14; Harold E. Turley 1934-35; Joe L. Turner 1985-88; John M. Turner 1936; John W. Turner, Jr. 1930.

U Calvin H. Udall 1945, Morris K. Udall 1942, 1947-48; Stewart Lee Udall 1939-40, 1946; John A. Ugrin 1969, 1971; Howard Lawrence Talcott Underhill 1911-12.

V Thomas A. Van Atta 1955; James Van Coevering 1969-70, Robert E. Van Dusan 1923; Jack R. Van Hook 1936; Mitchell Swick Vialo 1930; Elmer Francis Vickers, Jr. 1934-36; John Vlahogeorge 1982.

W Joseph William Wagner 1955-56; James H. Wakefield 1973-74; Rickey Walker 1982; Thomas Jay Wallace 1918-22; Charles N. Walters 1936; Ralph Elmo Warford 1935-37; William Warner 1969-71; Harold Charles Warnock 1932-34; Herbert A. Washington 1907; Wilber C. Webb 1930; Charles Wm. Weese 1960-61; Rex M. Welton 1967-69; Leslie Westfall 1940-42; Bruce M. Wheatley 1986; Brian C. Williams 1990-91; Corey Williams 1993-96; Peter Williams 1984-85; Thomas Williams 1977-78; Gordon Kenneth Wilson 1954; Puntus Wilson 1983; Ralph Curtis Winters 1935; Hugh M. Wolfin 1907; Wayne Womack 1989-92; Oslie Leon Wood III 1980; Charles Edwards Wooddell 1905; Emil K. Wuerderman 1905; Walter Henry Wuerderman 1910.

Y Robert Kirk Young 1960-62; Dan Yurkovich 1945.

Z Miles Murton Zeller 1959; Michael G. Zeno 1979.

TRIVIA ANSWERS

1. Morris Udall by Denver in 1948.

2. "Fritz"

3. Herring Hall, Bear Down Gym, Tucson High School, Tucson Community Center, McKale Center.

4. Arizona, Arizona State, Northern Arizona, New Mexico State, New Mexico, Texas Tech, UTEP, West Texas State and Hardin-Simmons.

5. The streak started with a win Dec. 14, 1945, over Williams Air Force Base. Kansas State broke the streak on Dec. 8, 1952.

6. Hadie Redd, 1951-52

7. As a baseball player, Snowden possessed a scrappy determination to reach base. He was also an intelligent base runner.

8. Kansas State's Jack Hartman

9. San Diego State, Northern Arizona, Florida International, Stanford.

10. Michael Tait, Pete Williams, Eddie Smith, Keith Jackson and Brock Brunkhorst.

11. James H. Pierce

12. The 1945-46 team played Kentucky during the NIT at Madison Square Garden. Arizona lost 77-53.

13. Link Richmond

14. Morris (Mo) was a combination forward/center, while Stewart was a guard.

15. Bill Reeves, 1955-57

16. 1958-59 with a 4-22 record.

17. Cedric Dempsey

18. The 1972 recruiting class of Eric Money, Coniel Norman, Jim Rappis and John Irving.

19. Frank Smith

20. The Year 2000